TO
BRIGHTON

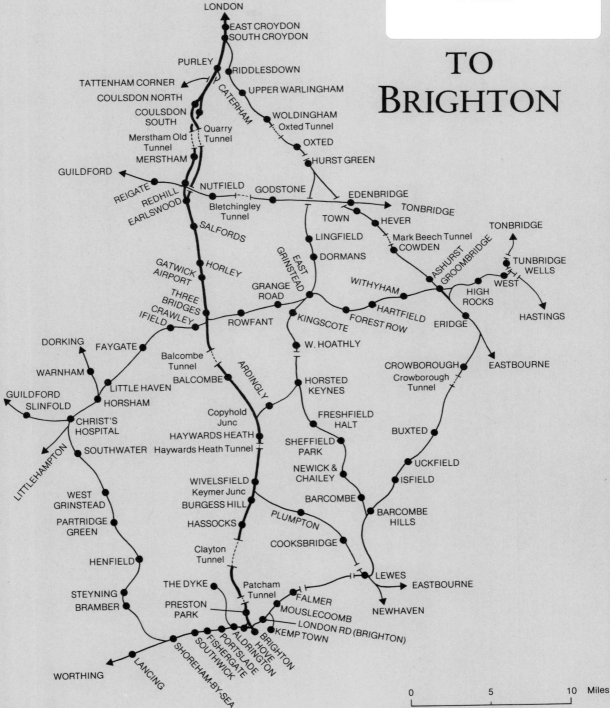

LONDON

EAST CROYDON
SOUTH CROYDON

PURLEY
RIDDLESDOWN

TATTENHAM CORNER
COULSDON NORTH
UPPER WARLINGHAM
CATERHAM
COULSDON
SOUTH
WOLDINGHAM
Oxted Tunnel
Quarry
Tunnel
Merstham Old
Tunnel
OXTED
MERSTHAM
HURST GREEN

GUILDFORD
NUTFIELD
GODSTONE
EDENBRIDGE
REIGATE
REDHILL
TONBRIDGE
EARLSWOOD
Bletchingley
Tunnel
TOWN
HEVER
SALFORDS
LINGFIELD
Mark Beech Tunnel
TONBRIDGE
COWDEN
GATWICK
AIRPORT
HORLEY
DORMANS
ASHURST
GROOMBRIDGE
TUNBRIDGE
WELLS
EAST
GRINSTEAD
WEST
THREE
BRIDGES
GRANGE
ROAD
WITHYHAM
HIGH
ROCKS
CRAWLEY
ROWFANT
HARTFIELD
IFIELD
KINGSCOTE
FOREST ROW
ERIDGE
HASTINGS
FAYGATE
W. HOATHLY
DORKING
Balcombe
Tunnel
CROWBOROUGH
WARNHAM
BALCOMBE
ARDINGLY
Crowborough
Tunnel
EASTBOURNE
LITTLE HAVEN
GUILDFORD
SLINFOLD
HORSHAM
HORSTED
KEYNES
CHRIST'S
HOSPITAL
Copyhold
Junc
FRESHFIELD
HALT
BUXTED
HAYWARDS HEATH
SOUTHWATER
Haywards Heath Tunnel
SHEFFIELD
PARK
UCKFIELD
LITTLEHAMPTON
WIVELSFIELD
NEWICK &
CHAILEY
ISFIELD
Keymer Junc
WEST
GRINSTEAD
BURGESS HILL
BARCOMBE
PARTRIDGE
GREEN
HASSOCKS
PLUMPTON
BARCOMBE
HILLS
Clayton
Tunnel
COOKSBRIDGE
HENFIELD
LEWES
THE DYKE
Patcham
Tunnel
EASTBOURNE
STEYNING
FALMER
BRAMBER
PRESTON
PARK
MOUSLECOOMB
NEWHAVEN
LONDON RD (BRIGHTON)
BRIGHTON
KEMP TOWN
HOVE
ALDRINGTON
PORTSLADE
FISHERGATE
SOUTHWICK
WORTHING
LANCING
SHOREHAM-BY-SEA

0   5   10   Miles

LONDON
TO
BRIGHTON

By the same author
Picture Reference Book of Railways
Irish Railways since 1916
Journey to Katmandu
The Railways of the Republic of Ireland
Sussex Villages
Sussex Scenes
Vintage Train
The Changing Southern Scene
The Changing London Midland Scene
The Changing Western Scene
Dorset
Great Western Tribute
Steam Echoes
The Waterloo to Weymouth Line

LONDON
TO
BRIGHTON

150 years of Britain's premier holiday line

Michael H.C. Baker

Patrick Stephens Limited

For Caroline Jacob and all the staff at Brighton Reference Library

First published in 1989

British Library Cataloguing in Publication Data
Baker, Michael, *1937-*
London to Brighton: 150 years of Britain's
premier holiday line.
1. South-east England. Railway services:
British rail. Southern region. London-
Brighton line, to 1982
I. Title
385'.09422

ISBN 1-85260-146-9

Patrick Stephens Limited is part of the Thorsons Publishing Group, Wellingborough, Northamptonshire NN8 2RQ, England.

Printed by Butler & Tanner Limited, Frome, Somerset

10 9 8 7 6 5 4 3 2 1

CONTENTS

PREFACE

The Brighton was the first railway line I ever travelled on, so for me it is a bit special. Mind you, there was a time when it was the least special of all lines simply because it was so familiar. Nearly all the trains which worked it were the least interesting of trains, electric multiple units. The fact that they were efficient, clean, up-to-date and reliable cut little ice. They didn't have separate locomotives, they weren't steam, they didn't have names, and they were all the same colour.

A small boy's view of the world is highly subjective, and not for one minute would I suggest that mine of the Brighton main line around the end of the Second World War is of much use to historians, and certainly none at all to statisticians. Nevertheless it was a view. And although we shall be bombarded with statistics, facts, figures and dates during our journey down the Brighton line through the pages of this book, accurate though I hope they are, they will not tell anything like the complete story.

For the Brighton is a line which has been and continues to be seen through many eyes. And to no two pairs is it quite identical. To Queen Victoria it was the means of so lowering the tone of Brighton that she abandoned her palace there, never to return. To those same masses who lowered its tone, the railway provided a means of reaching the seaside and enjoying its delights on a scale undreamed of in previous generations. To Arnold Bennett's Edwin Clayhanger, the Pullman which took him to Brighton was a 'gilded vehicle' with a 'vast interior', depositing him in a magnificent town 'vaster than any imagining of it'. Such wonder may have escaped generations of commuters to whom the line is merely a means of getting to and from work, a convenient enough one most of the time, but something upon which abuse is heaped whenever anything goes wrong. To the stage-coach operator of the early 1840s, the railway was the cause of his bankruptcy, to the motor coach operator of the 1920s and '30s it was the source of his livelihood if he could tempt enough of its passengers away from it.

Then there are the famous and not so famous theatricals, the racegoers, the airline passengers and crews, the cross-channel seafarers, the trainspotters, the school-children, to say nothing of the generations of railwaymen who have worked in all their

Brighton line luxury – the preserved first class 'Brighton Belle' Pullman car 'Audrey'.

myriad capacities on the line for 150 years.

Brighton is the most cosmopolitan of British resorts, elegant and scruffy, rich and poor, intellectually stimulating and vulgar, almost within sight of mainland Europe yet less than an hour from London. It is snobbish and generous, a town of elegant squares, within sight of the South Downs and windmills, yet the only town in the South of England which in parts might be mistaken for a Lancashire cotton town. All this bewildering variety is reflected in the railway which serves it.

*   *   *

'One of Brighton's most perfect attributes in the estimation of the majority of visitors is the ease with which it may be reached from any part of the United Kingdom. There are through trains from the Midlands, North, and West, whilst its proximity to London is well-known. Soon the present splendid train service will be augmented to the extent of there being several trains an hour in each direction between London and Brighton, on completion of the Southern Railway's electrification scheme, which will be the event of 1933, not only from the point of view of Brighton itself, but in the eyes of Londoners, who will be enabled to pay even more visits to Brighton than before. Such a contingency is to be welcomed with its prospect of the added fitness of Londoners as the result of their breathing the glorious sea breezes of Brighton with greater frequency.'

So wrote Maxwell Fraser in the 1932 official guidebook to Brighton. From the very beginning of their 150-year-old association, the fortunes of Brighton and its railway have been inextricably linked, and that link has encompassed a third partner, London. Although Brighton welcomes anyone from anywhere, and today the regular train service to destinations beyond the capital is more comprehensive than it has ever been, the title 'London by the Sea' is no idle boast.

In a quite hilarious foreword to the aforementioned guidebook, the Marquess of Donegal informs us that 'As I go about in London I hear young people of all ages discussing what fun it was last week-end. Where? The answer is always: "Oh, we went down to Brighton and met lots of amusing people." Brighton will go on having gayer and gayer week-ends. Just lately people who are well-known in London have been giving parties at Brighton in the same way as they used to at Le Touquet.'

H'm well, yes, no doubt, although one wonders whether that class of client existed in sufficient numbers to make an appreciable difference to the profits of either the Southern Railway or the Brighton holiday business. It was essentially the ordinary citizen, the City clerk, the department store assistant, the stevedore, the tradesman and his family, who were enabled by the railway to discover the glories of the seaside. Brighton was the first seaside resort, it was the first to be linked by train with London and it has always had the most comprehensive and frequent service.

And yet, as the Marquess implied, the railway was not simply a provider of transport for the masses. Brighton is the most cosmopolitan of seaside places and for 100 years the fortunes of that epitome of luxurious travel, the Pullman car, were inextricably linked with those of the Brighton line. The Pullman car company had its works between Preston Park and Brighton stations, and the world's first all-electric Pullman train, the 'Brighton Belle', ran for almost 40 years. Although its withdrawal in 1972 brought to an end, at least for the time being, the story of Pullmans on the Brighton line, all 15 of its cars have been preserved, two of them in the Preston Park works which is now a restoration centre.

Whilst the Brighton line was to become the jewel in the sparkling crown of the largest electrified network in the world, it was also long celebrated for its steam engines, not least because they were painted bright yellow. That livery disappeared around the turn of the century, although, like much else, the preservation movement has ensured its return. Brighton locomotives were remarkably long lived; in the latter years of steam, Stroudley's 'Terriers' were the oldest working survivors on British Railways, Britain's last 'Atlantics' were Marsh's distinguished 'H2s', whilst the workaday Billinton 0–6–2Ts and 0–6–0s seemed destined to go on for ever.

Elsewhere, once-grand seaside stations may be long past their heyday, but Brighton's, which is surely the most handsome in the land, is as busy as ever and in a magnificent state of repair. Insensitive management and greedy developers threatened its superb vaulted iron and glass roof some years ago but, after a fight, the battle seems to have been won.

Like so many of the world's great nineteenth-century railway stations, its design owes much to the Crystal Palace, and it was the re-erection of that building on Sydenham Heights after the Great Exhibition of 1851 which provided a boost to the Brighton railway's suburban traffic and led to the building of its West End terminus, Victoria. The Brighton railway is unusual in having two big London termini. For many years it shared both London Bridge and Victoria with other companies, not always amicably, but the greatest battle the London, Brighton & South Coast Railway fought — and won — was to retain its monopoly of Brighton.

It is a curious thing that John Saxby, who was one of the most innovative and successful of all railway engineers, should be relatively unknown. John Saxby was born in Brighton, began work with the London, Brighton & South Coast Railway and by the 1860s had pushed the company to the very forefront of signalling technology. The Brighton line and Saxby led the world. Saxby set up his own firm, took a partner, John Farmer, former Assistant Traffic Manager of the LB&SCR, and became the supplier to railways throughout the world. After a very long career, including a period in his late 60s and early 70s when he ran the French subsidiary of Saxby and Farmer, John Saxby retired to Sussex and died at the age of 89 in 1911.

Neither charabancs, baby Austins, motorways, nor the free-for-all motor coach competition of today have been able to make a significant impact on the Brighton line's prosperity. It has never been noted for high speed, but the relatively unimpeded access its trains enjoy both into Brighton and, most importantly, to the heart of the West End and to within a river's width of the City of London, are priceless assets which can only increase as road congestion grows.

RAILWAY CHRONICLE

TRAVELLING CHARTS;

Or, IRON ROAD BOOKS,

FOR PERUSAL ON THE JOURNEY:

IN WHICH ARE NOTED

THE TOWNS, VILLAGES, CHURCHES, MANSIONS, PARKS, STATIONS, BRIDGES, VIADUCTS, TUNNELS, CUTTINGS, GRADIENTS, &c., THE SCENERY AND ITS NATURAL HISTORY, THE ANTIQUITIES AND THEIR HISTORICAL ASSOCIATIONS, &c. PASSED BY THE LINE OF RAILWAY.

With numerous Illustrations.

Constituting a Novel and Complete Companion for the Railway Carriage.

[This Series of Papers is Copyright under 5 & 6 Vict. c. 45, and any infringement of it will be prosecuted]

LONDON AND BRIGHTON.

[SECOND EDITION.]

(circa 1845)

TERMINUS OF THE BRIGHTON, DOVER AND CROYDON RAILWAYS AT LONDON BRIDGE.

THE BEGINNING OF BRIGHTON

One wouldn't think that a tome with the gripping title of *A Dissertation Concerning the Use of Sea-Water in Diseases of the Glands* would have brought into existence the finest resort in the country and Pullman trains pulled by bright yellow engines — well, bright yellow ochre engines — but it did.

In the days when Brighton was merely a fishing village called Brighthelmstone, Lewes, eight miles distant across the Downs, was an ancient and important town, where Simon de Montfort, the founder of English democracy, won one of the bloodiest battles in our history; almost 600 years later in 1845, more than a wagonload of bone fragments was carted away when the railway line between Lewes and Brighton was being excavated through the site of the Battle of Lewes. Between 1555 and 1557, Mary Tudor had 17 Protestants burned at the stake in Lewes. This cataclysmic event was still marked each 5 November in the last century by ritual burnings of effigies of the Pope and a good deal of anti-Roman Catholic feeling, and the railway company played its part, unwittingly, in one of the worst Bonfire night excesses. The line between Lewes and Brighton had opened in 1846, and the following year a particularly large number of 'revellers', many brought in by train, had to be read the Riot Act on the steps of the Town Hall. And this despite the presence of a detachment of police from London, also conveyed by train.

One of Lewes's residents during the reign of George II was Dr Richard Russell, who had been born in the town in November 1687. It was he who published the abovementioned dissertation on sea-water in 1750. The essence of it was that salt-water possessed powerful healing properties. Now this was hardly news, for the medical profession had known it for generations, but Dr Russell's opus appeared just as public interest in such matters was on the increase. He started sending his patients to Brighthelmstone, not merely to bathe in the sea but also to drink the salt-water, in carefully regulated doses. Not surprisingly, some baulked at the notion of being dipped into the chilly waters, for the cure was not confined to the summer months. To help them overcome their reluctance, local people were employed as 'Dippers'. Their function was to take a firm grip upon the reluctant bathers — it was, after all, for their own good — haul them out of their wheeled bathing chariots, the forerunners of bathing machines, and plunge them into the English Channel. Grabbing hold of a high-born scruff of the neck — even royalty submitted itself to such treatment — and manhandling it under the waves must have been even better than taking part in the French Revolution; all the satisfaction of getting one over on the nobs, with none of the risk of retribution.

Russell moved to Brighthelmstone, into its largest house, in 1753. By the time he died, on a visit to London in 1759, the visitors were crowding in to drink water, first from the sea and later from the Chalybeate Spring in what is now St Ann's Well Gardens, Hove, and to bathe.

Six years after Russell's death, Brighthelmstone received its first royal visitor, the younger brother of George III. Royal patronage always did the trick in establishing a resort's status, as Brighton's neighbours, Worthing and Bognor, would affirm, and the final confirmation of Brighthelmstone's elevation from fishing village to playground of the rich and privileged came with the arrival of the Prince Regent in 1783. The term 'Regency Brighton' was about to enter the history books.

Brighton's railway station is very fine, but even its most ardent admirers would have to admit that it is merely one of hundreds of splendid edifices in Georgian, Regency and various Victorian styles with which the town is endowed, the most famous of which — indeed the most famous piece of seaside architecture in the British Isles — is the Royal Pavilion. This was leased by the Prince Regent in 1786 for Mrs Fitzherbert. At that stage in its career it was a perfectly ordinary farmhouse owned by the Kemp family, who were lords of the manor (hence the Kemp Town area of the town which would be later served by its own branch line). The Prince Regent set about the first of a series of rebuildings which finally, in 1822, after John Nash had been let loose upon it, resulted in the extraordinary riot of 'Hindoo' domes, pinnacles and columns which have proved such a delight down the generations.

The Royal Pavilion is a good quarter of a mile from the sea, and even Dr Russell made sure his front door faced away from the beach, for in those days it simply wasn't done to have a residence overlooking the water — unless, of course, one was a fisherman, when one had little choice. Thus the Royal Crescent, erected between 1799 and 1807 on the East Cliffs and facing boldly out to sea, was considered amazingly daring. Perhaps the fact that the

Crescent was the responsibility of a West Indian, J. B. Otto, who presumably had less inhibitions about seaside residences, had something to do with it. (Mr Otto commissioned from one Rossi a statue which was unique in that it was meant to be of the Prince Regent but was frequently mistaken for Lord Nelson on account of one arm and other important bits having fallen off.)

What with its sea water cures, Royal Pavilion and elegant terraces, its racecourse and crumbling statues, Brighton in the years after the Napoleonic wars was quite the place to be: no one called it Brighthelmstone any more. The London road, by way of Reigate and Cuckfield, had been macadamized, and such was the competition over its 53 miles that no fewer than 52 stage-coaches regularly vied for the business which was generated. Coach horses were changed every ten miles and as a consequence the time for the overall journey was a little over $3\frac{1}{2}$ hours. This was astonishingly fast, and the young bucks loved to race each other; the day trip to the seaside had arrived. But if horsepower could do this well, think what steam might achieve . . .

One does not today associate Brighton with regular cross-Channel travel, but in fact the town was long a port for France and a regular service of sailing ships to and from Dieppe had begun in 1792. In the year of Waterloo — the battle, not the station — steam boats began to operate on the Thames. In 1824, the

The Royal Pavilion from a watercolour by W.H. Borrow.

General Steam Navigation Company started to operate paddle-steamers between Brighton and Dieppe, by which time a host of services connected the capital with various Thames estuary and south coast towns; steam had arrived in Brighton.

On the day the railway between Shoreham and Brighton opened, the *Brighton Gazette* noted that the GSNC packet *Dart* had just completed its maiden voyage from Greenwich to Brighton. This took 13 hours, which was vastly longer than the stagecoach, to say nothing of what the railway would be able to achieve when the London to Brighton line opened a year later. Nevertheless, *Dart* received much praise, its 120 horsepower engines and its general appointments being far superior to those of its predecessors. The sea distance between Greenwich and Brighton is 160 miles, which meant that *Dart* had achieved a highly commendable average of 12 mph; it had taken three hours from Hastings. To facilitate boarding and disembarking from the ships, a suspension pier, the Chain Pier, was built. It was immortalized in 1828 by Turner who had a studio at Petworth House, the home of the third Lord Egremont. Egremont did much to encourage both Turner and Constable, and was an original shareholder in the Chain Pier. A sketch of Turner's painting rests in the Tate Gallery, whilst the finished version can be seen in Petworth House.

Once the train had established itself the steamship service was wound up, although elsewhere coastal passenger services lasted much longer; those from London to Dundee and Liverpool, for example, survived into the twentieth century.

ORIGINS

The origins of what would eventually become the London to Brighton line have, in fact, little to do with the latter town itself, although they are concerned with London and the sea. During the last decade of the eighteenth and the first of the nineteenth centuries, the whole of southern England was bracing itself for an invasion by Napoleon. Improvements in communications between London and the coast, and particularly the great naval base of Portsmouth, were continuously sought; out of these came proposals for a canal. It was to start from the Thames at Wandsworth and follow the course of the river Wandle as far as Croydon — where the Archbishop of Canterbury had his country residence — and then head seawards through the North Downs. The iron industry flourished hereabouts, as it had for centuries in the heavily wooded Weald of Surrey, Sussex and Kent, and this would greatly benefit from a better transport system. In the event, the idea of a canal was given up in favour of that of a railway, and on 21 May 1801 the Surrey Iron Railway was incorporated.

It was opened on 26 July 1803, and was in most respects like the mineral railways already in existence in the north. But in one most important respect it was different. It was a public, not a private railway, and anyone who had a suitable wagon could run it upon the tracks. It was the first railway of any sort south of the Thames, although it was, more accurately, a plateway, being laid with plate rails fixed on stone blocks. The iron-tyred wheels of the wagons were flangeless, as on all plateways, and the wagons were pulled by horses. Tolls were charged, based upon the distance the goods were to travel, their weight and their nature.

The next stage of the line, known as the Croydon, Merstham and Godstone Iron Railway, was opened in 1805. This continued south through Purley to Merstham, where there was a gap in the North Downs and a lime works. 1805 was also the year of Trafalgar, and Nelson's victory over the French fleet had a direct bearing on the railway. The likelihood of invasion was now much diminished, and the need for a railway or canal between London and Portsmouth was thus less urgent. The most difficult and expensive section through the Downs still lay ahead, so it was decided to proceed no further; the Merstham gap became the

Two of the very few relics of the Surrey Iron Railway still surviving: a couple of plate rails which have been on display for many years in the Rectory Field, Purley, on the opposite side of the valley from where the present main line runs.

terminus of the railway. Between Wandsworth and Croydon the line was double, from there southwards it was single.

One of the reasons for building a railway rather than a canal along the valley of the Wandle was that the latter would have reduced the water level in the river. This was important, not for navigation, but for the many industrial processes such as brewing, textile processing and iron production which went on in the valley. Nevertheless, these pre-Industrial Revolution enterprises were on a small scale and the traffic they generated between Croydon and the Thames at Wandsworth was limited.

The Merstham extension fared a little better. Apart from the lime works there was, as there is today, a fuller's earth works at Redhill, and for a while the line was quite busy. In 1824, George Valentine Hall took over the lime works. He was to found the firm of Hall and Company which, in later years, established its offices and depot beside East Croydon station. In British Railways' days, a small diesel painted in Hall's bright red livery shunted the depot sidings. Ready Mixed Concrete took over Hall and Co around 1960, orange replaced red and the rail connection disappeared. It was pleasant, however, to see one of the once-familiar pre-war Bedford lorries sporting its original colours on display during a vintage vehicle rally in the station yard at Sheffield Park a couple of years back.

A small, but interesting, exhibition to mark the 175th anniversary of the Surrey Iron Railway was held by Croydon Library in the summer of 1978. Inevitably not much of the railway is left, but its route can be traced, notably the section along the edge of Mitcham Common, where the single-track West Croydon to Wimbledon line now runs, and Tramway Path and Factory Lane in West Croydon. The line ended at Pitlake, near to what is now Wandle Park. The district is still heavily industrial, dominated by the vast towers of the Beddington Lane power station erected in the late 1940s, although the gas works, which gave the district such a pungent aroma — we were told it was good for your health but I'm glad I didn't live near enough to find out — has gone.

A short stretch of line linked the Pitlake terminus of the Surrey Iron Railway with the Croydon Canal, which ran northwards to Deptford where it, in turn, connected with the Grand Surrey Canal. This, despite its title, was a very minor affair rather less than three miles in length, running from Camberwell through Deptford to the Thames with a branch to Peckham. The Croydon Canal was later to form the trackbed of the London and Croydon Railway, and the Croydon, Merstham and Godstone Railway was similarly reincarnated when some of its lands were used by the continuation of the line towards Brighton. The Croydon, Merstham and Godstone closed between 1838 and 1840, and the Surrey Iron Railway in 1846. There were proposals that the Brighton line might use its track bed and make a

A Bedford drop-side lorry built for Hall & Co of Croydon in 1934.

*A footbridge spanning the
West Croydon to Sutton
and Wimbledon lines where
the Surrey Iron Railway
once ran at Wandle Park,
Pitlake, Croydon.*

junction with the London & South Western near the site of the
present Earlsfield station and share the LSWR's Waterloo terminus, but these came to nothing.

Neither of the pioneer railways was ever worked by any
mechanical means. Some of the earthworks of the Merstham line
survived until the building of the M23, but the vast Spaghetti
Junction-like interchange with the M25 at Merstham obliterated
most traces. As Derek A. Bayliss, in an article in *Railway
Magazine* in July 1978, records, two wagon wheels were fished
out of the Wandle at Mitcham some 20 years ago and one is on
display in Guildford Museum. Pieces of rail have also been
recovered from time to time, and no doubt descendants of the
horses which once provided the motive power for the world's first
public railway are going about their business, presumably
unaware of their distinguished pedigree.

THE CROYDON RAILWAY

East Croydon has long been the busiest intermediate station between London and Brighton, and although not quite all trains stop there — the Victoria to Gatwick expresses, for example — it is much the most important.

Croydon has a long history. It was once a centre of the charcoal-burning industry which flourished in the densely wooded weald of Surrey, Sussex and Kent. There is a Colliers Water Lane deep in the heart of suburban Thornton Heath, miles from any twentieth-century forest, which gave its name, briefly, to Thornton Heath station when this opened in 1862. Collier is a trade description much older than the industrial revolution. In medieval times, fuel for London came from the Croydon area and there was actually a play performed for Queen Elizabeth, who of course visited Croydon along with just about everywhere else, which was called 'Grim, the collyer of Croydone'.

The Wandle, which rises in South Croydon, is only 11 miles long and was never navigable, but it was a river of importance, at least locally, for in the eighteenth century in that 11 miles it powered no fewer than 68 water wheels. Basil E. Cracknell, in his *Portrait of Surrey*, describes it at that time as 'one of the busiest rivers in the world'. Hard to believe now, when for much of its length it seems no grander than a glorified sewer, but nevertheless quite true. It was picturesque, too; John Ruskin, who did more than any other Victorian to awake the growing middle class to the beauties and the great variety of nature within the British Isles, praised the Wandle. Perhaps that is why a boys' grammar school which used to be within a few hundred yards of the Surrey Iron Railway's Pitlake terminus was named after him.

Croydon's parish church, down in Old Town, is the successor of a church which was a hundred years old at the time of Domesday, but the only really old buildings in the centre of Croydon today are the Whitgift almshouses, an extraordinary Tudor flintstone survival sandwiched between the fast food and office supply emporia; although the antiquated state of East Croydon station might suggest that that establishment is scarcely more modern.

We have seen that by the first decade of the nineteenth century Croydon was linked to the Thames by a canal and a railway; both were pretty primitive affairs and neither carried passengers. It was inevitable that the first proper railway south of London would head for Croydon, and thus the Act for the Croydon Railway received the Royal Assent on 12 June 1835. No one in the early days of railways was quite sure how great should be their ambitions and whether those they had would be achieved, and a cautious Parliament decreed that one London terminus would be quite sufficient on the south side of the Thames.

Thus the Croydon Railway had to share London Bridge station with the London & Greenwich Railway, which had opened on 14 December 1836, the very first railway in London. Although it was only 3¾ miles long the London & Greenwich had done great business from the start. This was much to the surprise of George Landmann, the engineer, who was so pessimistic about his railway's prospects that he felt the only chance of covering its cost was to let off as many of the arches on which it was carried as possible for dwelling houses, as well as commerical premises. In fact, despite being high above the streets and tenements for virtually its entire length, the cost of building the approach to London Bridge and the station itself had not been excessive.

The immediate area around London Bridge was heavily built up, but there were still fields within 400 yards, and the Greenwich line ran mostly through market gardens. A good deal of the land was owned by the church; in fact, the Bishops of Win-

Rush hour at London Bridge, 29 March 1978. Crompton diesel-electric No 33049 about to take out the 17.19 to Uckfield, whilst all around are suburban 4EPBs and 4SUBs, to the left on former SECR tracks, to the right on former LB & SCR ones.

chester, Rochester and London, and the Archbishop of Canterbury, had charge of most of the land upon which Cannon Street, Charing Cross and London Bridge stations and the lines leading to them were built. It has been suggested that the Church had been so willing to sell, and to sell so cheaply, to the railway companies because it was ashamed of owning slum property. Would that all nineteenth-century landlords had been as conscience stricken. It is certainly true that there were some appalling slums in this area of London, and perhaps a brand new home inside a railway arch would have been preferable to the conditions which many families endured in early Victorian times, but few took up the offer.

The Greenwich trains had far less distance to travel than the Thames steamers with which they competed, and they caused the latter's operators to cut their fares drastically in a vain attempt to stave off bankruptcy. Until the railway appeared the boats had only to worry about omnibuses and their own poor safety record; between May 1835 and November 1838, 12 boats were severely damaged in accidents and 43 persons were drowned. However, London streets were far from safe, or clean, and as the boats were as fast as the omnibuses as well as cheaper, demand was such that they ran every half-hour between Westminster and Greenwich in winter, every quarter-hour in summer. The journey to Woolwich took $1\frac{1}{4}$ hours, a quarter of an hour longer if the boats had the tide against them. The fare was one shilling (5p) inside, 9d ($3\frac{1}{2}$p) outside.

*Greenwich station. A train
from Charing Cross and
London Bridge is departing
from the down platform.*

George Shillibeer had put his first omnibus on the streets of London in 1829. Although an Englishman and a former lieutenant in the Royal Navy, Shillibeer's French connections were many and he operated his first bus in Nantes, in 1827. The omnibus was a wonderful thing. With vastly greater capacity than a stage-coach, seats did not have to be pre-booked; it also 'liberated thousands from the extortions of the cabmen', to quote O. J. Morris. Although cheap, it was highly respectable, and was as much a classless form of travel as the train. It put into men's, and young ladies', heads the notion that one no longer had to live within walking distance of one's place of work. The railway companies, of course, capitalized on this notion, none more enthusiastically than the Brighton line. Shillibeer, after making a fortune, lost it when he extended his empire out to Greenwich and Woolwich shortly before the railway opened and took most of his, and the steamboats', passengers.

Spa Road, Bermondsey, had been the temporary terminus of trains from Greenwich and it was not until the end of 1836 that London Bridge was ready; the Lord Mayor and Corporation of London, together with the Secondary and High Bailiff of Southwark, performed the opening ceremony on 14 December.

Currey and Smith were the station's architects, and, as opened, its two platforms were totally without covering. In the cellars beneath them wine was stored, recently arrived from Spain and

Portugal by way of Hays Wharf across Tooley Street.

Croydon Railway trains began to run into London Bridge on 5 June 1839, four days after the opening of the Croydon line. They had to share the Greenwich Railway tracks for the $1\frac{3}{4}$ miles from the junction at Corbet's Lane, Rotherhithe, and to accommodate them two more platforms were built at the terminus, north of the Greenwich ones. Corbett's (nowadays it has an extra 't') Lane Junction is a landmark in railway history, for it was here that the first signal box was erected. Not only that, but the first colour light signalling was also installed here: 'powerful parabolical reflectors from which signals by coloured lights can be given a long way off to approaching trains, so as to prevent the chance of collision'. And to cap it all, Hutton Gregory, the company's engineer, invented semaphore signals. These were set up at stations, and in the horizontal position indicated STOP, at 45 degrees GO SLOWLY and when vertical, hidden inside the post, GO. The system was a great improvement, both on the policeman universally employed from the beginnings of railways and the many other mechanical systems then being experimented with.

Saxby signalboxes on the SER at London bridge circa 1866.

Semaphores still in evidence over a century later at West Croydon; a two-coach train from Wimbledon arrives, having just traversed part of the route of the Surrey Iron Railway.

From Corbet's Lane Junction, the line swung due south to New Cross. Here it settled itself into the bed of the Croydon Canal, which had been bought for £50,250 — and then drained. However, a good deal more than just letting out the water had to be done before rails could be laid. For a start, there were the 28 locks which carried it up to the heights of Forest Hill and Sydenham and back down again. These were replaced with a deep cutting through the clay soil where, not surprisingly, earth slips gave trouble from time to time. From New Cross, a $2\frac{3}{4}$ miles-long bank at 1 in 100 confronted southbound trains. It was a tremendous obstacle, and in order to get round the limited power of the steam locomotives of the time the company decided on a revolutionary solution. It would have an atmospheric railway.

The principle of this, as is well known, was that trains were connected by a piston to a pipe set between the running rails. This pipe was sealed so that air could be drawn out ahead of the piston and the resulting vacuum would move the piston and the train along. Had it worked it would have been the least polluting mode of transport yet devised, even if it would have killed the engine number collecting hobby before it got started.

Cubitt, somewhat reluctantly, agreed to its installation and the first section opened between Forest Hill and Croydon in August 1845 for trials, and to the public in January of the following year. The New Cross to Forest Hill section followed early in 1847.

However, as with all atmospheric railways, the technology of the time was not up to the brilliance of the idea, it proved impossible to maintain the vacuum and without this there was no power. Not the least of the system's problems was pointwork — no practical way was ever worked out of devising points and crossovers. The only possible answer seemed to be to carry one line over the other by a bridge. In years to come, in heavily trafficked areas, flyovers and underpasses would become commonplace, but the need for them was hardly realized in those early days.

Thus it was that the world's first railway flyover was constructed at the Jolly Sailor near Norwood Junction. This carried the West Croydon line over the East Croydon one. By 1847, the original Croydon station was no longer a terminus, for an extension through Carshalton and Wallington to Epsom had been opened. It had been intended that this also would be worked by atmospheric trains and, although it never was, the advantage to an increasingly intensive service of such a sophisticated means of making a junction was not lost. Others were subsequently built within the Norwood, Selhurst and Croydon triangle as well as at countless locations world-wide.

The distance from Corbet's Lane to Croydon was $8\frac{3}{4}$ miles, making the distance from end to end a neat 10 miles. The Croydon terminus was at what is now known as West Croydon, beside the Brighton road and a quarter of a mile north of the Whitgift almshouses. Croydon station was described as 'extensive' and 'excellently arranged' containing 'every comfort that can be desired'.

The beanfeast at the opening of the line on 1 June 1839 was as indulgently self-congratulatory as could be managed; it was held at Croydon, but not before New Cross had been visited, where a band played in the engine-house. 'The effect from the reverberation of sound by the walls was truly grand', and anyone who has ever attended a concert at the Roundhouse in Camden will believe it.

The inaugural train, with the Lord Mayor of London as guest of honour, set out from London Bridge, reached Croydon in 31 minutes, this including an intermediate stop of $1\frac{3}{4}$ minutes, then returned to New Cross where directors from the Brighton, South Eastern and Greenwich railway companies joined it. After the reverberations, everyone then headed back to Croydon, stopping on the way to inspect the Dartmouth Arms and the Jolly Sailors. These were not, despite the directors' predilection for alcoholic celebrations, the public houses, but the stations named after them. The former is now Forest Hill, the latter Norwood Junction.

William Cubitt was the engineer and he had estimated that the total cost of the line would be £398,863 8s 9d. One may doubt whether he intended such a precise figure to be taken at its face value; one certainly hopes the directors didn't, for Cubitt overspent by £216,296 11s 3d, chiefly through unexpected problems with the deep cutting south of New Cross. The Cubitt family was famous in the pioneering days of railway engineering and rapidly became highly experienced. Brother Lewis was the architect of King's Cross, whilst brother Joseph was the engineer of the Great Northern Railway. For all that, it was easy enough to make an underestimate, but this one was monumental. However, it does not seem to have undermined the Croydon Railway's directors' faith in the Cubitt family, and Lewis was invited to design Bricklayers Arms station on a site selected by William. The family prospered and William eventually became Lord Mayor of London, whilst a nephew purchased the grandest country seat imaginable, the medieval Bodiam Castle, north of Hastings, complete with moat and drawbridge, and ended his days as Baron Ashcombe.

The public was allowed to begin regular travel on the Croydon Railway on 5 June 1839, and this it did with enthusiasm. There were 12 trains in each direction on weekdays, and only one less on Sundays. Right from the start, businessmen were catered for with a first class express leaving Croydon at 9.30 am and stopping only at Sydenham. All other trains stopped at all or most stations. An average of 1,812 passengers travelled each day in the first four months of the railway's existence, which was considered highly satisfactory, and probably necessary to counteract Mr Cubitt's inaccurate calculations. Fares that autumn were 2s (10p) first class, 1s 6d (7½p) second class. Initially there does not seem to have been any provision for third class passengers although they were being carried between Croydon and New Cross by the summer of 1842.

The railway started out with nine engines. Five were 2–2–2s built by Sharp, Roberts and Co, and there were two similar Rennie locomotives, one of which was named *Croydon*. Rennie also built two 0–4–2s which were provided chiefly to cope with the heavy climb up from New Cross. It is of interest that although the railway occupied the bed of a canal which had been exclusively a carrier of goods, initially there seems to have been little thought by the railway of anything other than passengers business. However, it did carry goods, for trials took place on New Cross bank with *Croydon* hauling five loaded coal wagons, and one of the 0–4–2s, *Hercules*, banking — 2–2–2 was a singularly unsuitable wheel arrangement for a goods engine.

The Town Hall gardens, site of Croydon Central station, closed in 1890.

We have now seen how the London end of the Brighton line originated, first with the Croydon Canal and the horse-drawn Surrey Iron and the Croydon, Merstham and Godstone railways, these being superseded by the London & Greenwich and the London & Croydon railways. Plans for several routes linking Brighton with the capital were being put forward as soon as steam railway travel was shown to be practical and it is to the realization of these that we will now turn our attention.

BRIGHTON TO SHOREHAM

In the 1830s Brighton was far and away the largest and most fashionable resort in Great Britain and it was still growing, although it was small by the standards of the industrial Midlands and North. The population rose from 24,500 in 1820 to over 40,000 in 1830 (Manchester's population was 142,000). Almost everyone who had either the time or the money, or both, liked to visit and be seen in Brighton, and in London there were soon vast numbers who fell into these categories. Thus it is not surprising that from the early 1820s numerous proposals had been put forward for railways between London and Brighton and that in the early 1830s six were being actively championed at vast expense. Their engineers ranged from the obscure to the famous — amongst the latter were Charles Vignoles, John Rennie and Robert Stephenson.

The London and Brighton Railway company came into existence on 15 July 1837, 25 days after Queen Victoria came to the throne, but it was a line Her Majesty would patronize only fitfully. She travelled it several times in her early days as Queen, before she abandoned the Royal Pavilion at Brighton, but seldom thereafter, preferring the LSWR route to reach Osborne on the Isle of Wight. Cecil Allen speculates that 'some discourteous treatment she received there in the early years of her reign' resulted in her antipathy both to Brighton and the Brighton railway. Nevertheless, the LB&SCR built a handsome Royal Train right at the end of her reign in the late 1890s which was used for journeys to the Derby at Epsom and to and from Portsmouth by various members of the royal family. Its most remarkable and celebrated run with Queen Victoria was actually after her death, when her body was brought back from Osborne to London in February 1901; but more of that anon.

There was fierce fighting, both within and without Parliament, over the financing and the route of the new line. None of the prepared routes precisely followed the Brighton road, and all had to contend with the North and South Downs. Stephenson was in favour of a line down the Mole valley beneath Boxhill to Dorking, on to the ancient town of Horsham and through the Adur gap to Shoreham, and indeed a railway would one day take this route. Sir John Rennie's route from Croydon, which would win the day, passed through Merstham, ran close to, but not through, Reigate, then on to Horley, close to, but not through, Crawley, through the depths of the great forest which covered most of Sussex, between Cuckfield and Lindfield, tunnelled boldly through the South Downs beneath the twin windmills at Ditchling, and so reached Brighton.

One MP, W. Crawford, asserted that 'the feeling against Rennie's line was all but universal from Wandsworth Common to Horsham'. He based this sweeping assertion on a few letters of complaint and the fact that the financial arrangements were not to his own advantage. There was much more in this vein but no one doubted that there would be a railway between London and Brighton and, in the event, Rennie and Stephenson reached a compromise and, at the third attempt, their scheme got through.

The Act stipulated that the line would run from a junction with the London & Croydon Railway near Norwood Junction straight through the Surrey and Sussex Weald to the sea. The precise description of the junction was 'at or near Selhurst Farm'. To anyone who knows Selhurst today, set deep in suburban Croydon, the notion of a farm within its boundaries must seem archaic, but as recently as 1950, when I was at school in Croydon, a schoolfriend and myself used to spend our winter Saturday afternoons in a pig farm, on account of the said farm being on the school cross-country course. We got to know one of the farm hands and would chat to him whilst rubbing the back of a pig and awaiting the appearance of the runners. He had a marked rural accent; we asked him where he came from, expec-

A view of the Brighton railway at the time of its opening (Brighton Library).

ting him to reply Devon or Derbyshire or somewhere equally rural and exotic. Not a bit of it. 'Lived in Croydon all me life, worked here since I was a boy.' His must have been just about the last true Croydon accent, as opposed to the South London one everyone I knew possessed. And this was just two miles from East Croydon station.

The coming of the railway would first disturb and then destroy the age old pattern of rural life which was still practised as close to London as New Cross and Clapham when the Brighton line was being planned. In 1865 there were two weekly markets in Croydon, one for cattle, the other for corn. They were extremely popular and buyers and sellers came from all over London and the south-east. The advent of the railway made travel to them much easier, but at the same time encouraged the sale of farm land for building, and there was thus less and less pasture for animals. For all that, the cattle market at South Croydon survived until 1935 whilst the famous fruit, vegetable and meat market in Surrey Street, midway between East and West Croydon stations, grew more popular and in 1922 became daily, as it still is.

Further south, beyond Coulsdon, agriculture would remain the principal industry and occupation for at least the rest of the century, although the presence of junctions at Redhill, Three Bridges and Haywards Heath would create towns where there had previously been only scattered cottages. As the twentieth century dawned, 60 years after the opening of the Brighton line, it was still commonplace to come across 'the old Sussex yeoman in his slate-coloured elaborately yoked and frilled smock coat, and his buttoned-up hip leggings and heavy hobnailed boots'. Up on the Downs, teams of great sure-footed, dark red Sussex oxen still ploughed the chalk soil. The soaring meat prices of the First World War, rather than mechanization, brought them to the edge of extinction, the last team being retired from Exceat, above Seaford, in 1925.

The London and Brighton Railway bought the virtually defunct Croydon, Merstham and Godstone Railway and made use of part of its track bed. John Rastrick was the engineer in charge, while David Mocatta, a vice-president of the Royal Institute of British Architects, was responsible for the stations. There was some delay between the passing of the Act and the start of work, as Rastrick decided to resurvey the route. This he did, and having produced a much more satisfactory line, on 12 July 1838 work began.

The navvies descended on Merstham and set to work excavating the cutting on the London side of the tunnel. They were tough, hard-working, hard-drinking men, recruited from all over the British Isles to do a back-breaking, dangerous job with virtually no mechanical assistance. I was recently watching a film of Chinese working on road and irrigation schemes during the Cultural Revolution of the 1960s and it struck me how vividly that horde of toiling humanity, using nothing but wooden wheelbarrows and hand-tools, evoked the Britain of a hundred and more years earlier when our railway system was being formed.

Over 6,000 men worked on the Brighton line. Perhaps the best remembered incident is the strike threat during the building of Merstham tunnel when it was discovered that the nearest beer was over two miles away, across the hills at Woodmansterne in the Chipstead Valley. Boys, paid $\frac{1}{2}$d a journey by the contractors, were employed to replenish supplies, and the crisis was averted. Down by the sea, the 'peaceable inhabitants of Portslade were greatly annoyed' when one wet day at the end of September 1838 200 navvies employed on the Brighton to Shoreham section, being unable to work, did their best to drink the town dry and got roaring drunk.

There is a painting of navvies at work on the Shoreham line in Brighton Museum by G. Smith dating from 1839. The men are digging a cutting and in the distance is the Adur estuary with the silhouette of Shoreham in front, a few buildings beside the sea closer in and a lone windmill opposite. For the rest there is nothing but open countryside. The only cutting on the line anywhere between Hove and Shoreham is beside the cemetery immediately east of Portslade station, and although this is rather shallower than in the picture, this is clearly the setting. How it has changed! The picture was commissioned by the directors of the railway company and presented to their chairman.

As the work continued, the *Sussex Express* faithfully reported its progress and from time to time published editorials and letters reflecting the attitudes of the Brighton townsfolk and other interested parties. These varied from the thoughtfully reasoned to the plan barmy. The paper itself commented, 'It is feared by some that it will be the means of bringing into the town a class of persons objectionable to the vistors of mode and fashion who are in the habit of resorting hither and thither and will not be disposed to mix with them . . . Our Marine Parade, the West Cliff and the Squares are composed of first rate mansions within the reach of none but the rich merchants or the aristocracy and we warrant that our public downs and walks have ample space and scope enough to prevent them mixing with our visitors of rank. The completion of the line will, it is confidentially contemplated by a

A contemporary engraving of the opening of the Shoreham Railway on 11 May 1840, with the inaugural train leaving Brighton station (Author's collection).

large majority of the inhabitants, be most beneficial to Brighton.' This may fairly be said to have represented the general view of the townsfolk, who have always viewed the future with a fair degree of confidence rather than, as in some seaside towns and resorts with pretentions to grandeur, looked back to an imagined era of stability when all was right with the world and everyone recognized his place in society and kept to it.

There were, of course, those who thought differently. The *Brighton Herald* published the following in February 1840: 'By some observations made by a Reverend Gentleman at a recent meeting it seems that another church is about to be erected under the auspices of the Vicar, at the North-Western part of the town — its object being to counteract the evil effects of the Railroad Terminus.' Perhaps the vicar had been reading Hansard and an exchange in the House of Commons between a Parliamentary Committee and a clergyman:

'You tell us that the railway navvies are mostly infidels. Would you say they are also socialists?'

'In practice, yes, because though most of them appear to have wives, few of them are really married.'

No doubt the voters who elected a Labour MP for Kemp Town in the 1960s, one of the very few ever to represent a seaside constituency, would have been highly incensed at this definition of a Socialist. It has to be said that there have been instances in

Brighton of persons living with other persons of the opposite sex to whom they were not married, and some of them were certainly not Socialists. (Well, at least I don't think the Prince Regent and Mrs Fitzherbert were . . .)

The first section of line to be completed was the six miles from Shoreham to Brighton. Shoreham is ancient and in Norman times was the principal port linking William the Conqueror's two kingdoms. King John came back through it from France after the death of Richard the Lionheart to claim the throne, and Charles II made his escape from Cromwell's men there. In the early 1800s Shoreham was Sussex's principal commercial port and thus it made good sense to start the railway from there and bring by sea much of the material needed for construction.

There was much discussion on where the terminus of the line at Brighton should be. Robert Stephenson proposed a site on the north side of Western Road and this was considered generally acceptable, although the residents of Brunswick Square, between Western Road and the sea, objected, fearing a loss of property values. The most convenient place would have been in the town centre north of the Pavilion and the Steine, on flat ground and within sight of the sea. Other seaside towns would have jumped at such a splendid site — we need think only of Blackpool, Morecambe and the old Ramsgate station — but the character of Brighton town centre would have been greatly changed and so, to avoid this and at great expense, a site was blasted out of the

Shoreham station and signal box, looking towards Worthing in March 1988.

hillside between Seven Dials and the London Road. Some 3,500 men and 1,570 horses were employed in the work which was completed ready for the opening on 11 May 1840.

The *Brighton Gazette and Lewes Observer* does not tell us what the weather was like, but we can assume it was not inclement for vast numbers stood out in the open air to watch. The inaugural train was due to leave the Brighton terminus at Trafalgar Street at 3 o'clock in the afternoon, but long before this excitement had reached fever pitch. The band of the 12th Lancers was on hand playing martial airs, whilst 'Those who had not been so fortunate as to obtain tickets congregated in the vicinity of the cutting, the New England Bridge, and the tunnel, being obliged to content themselves with such a knowledge of what was in progress as the occasional passage of an engine would give.'

The train consisted of six carriages, two for each class, each with seats for some 20 persons, and three luggage wagons especially fitted up with forms for the occasion; in all, 230 passengers were aboard. Mr Rastrick, the Engineer, Mr Harman, the Chairman, and other directors were 'assiduous in their attention'. The engine was *Kingston*, 'conducted by 'Jackson' (no title or christian name for a mere engine driver, even if he was the most important actor in the drama) who had been employed for the last 12 months in working *Brighton* and *Shoreham* for the removal of the earth along the line.

'Precisely at three o'clock the whistle was blown, and "all right" being answered by the waving of the white flag, the steam was turned on.' The train started but *Kingston*'s driving wheels slipped and the triumphal progress stopped before it had hardly begun. Mr Rastrick and others got down to investigate and it was discovered that the 'break' on a second class carriage had not been released. Just to make sure that nothing went wrong the next time, another engine, *Eagle*, was brought up to the rear of the train and with a hearty shove it got away 'with great velocity' 11 minutes late. Shoreham Harbour was passed at 3.21 and arrival at Shoreham station 'which is situate behind the Union Workshouse' was at 3.23. The five and a half mile run had taken 12 minutes, which was pretty good going.

Next day, Tuesday the 12th, regular services began. '1,750 persons paid the fare', many going on to the Swiss Gardens to a fete celebrating the line's opening. The third class single fare was 6d (2½p), second class 9d (3½p) and first class a shilling (5p). A first class coupé seat cost 1/6d (7½p). There was no doubting the enthusiasm of virtually the entire populace, and the *Brighton Gazette* 'confidently expected that Brighton would enter a new era of prosperity'. How right it was.

GREAT WORKS

Work on the main line between Brighton and Croydon was also progressing and the section as far south as Haywards Heath was ridden over by the inspectors on 28 June 1841. Two weeks later the public service over the $37\frac{3}{4}$ miles from London Bridge began. There were four trains in each direction on weekdays, and two on Sundays, averaging around two hours for the journey, then another two hours by coach to get to Brighton.

Rastrick's insistence on a fresh survey had paid dividends, for the line was extremely well engineered with a ruling gradient of 1 in 264 and no curvature of any significance. Between Croydon and Haywards Heath the line passed through two tunnels and one viaduct of note. The first of the tunnels, which was 1 mile 71 yards long, took the trains through the North Downs at Merstham. Deep in Balcombe Forest, $33\frac{1}{2}$ miles from London Bridge, was the 1,141 yards long Balcombe tunnel and immediately beyond it is what has become probably the best known feature on the entire line.

Hereabouts, the River Ouse, which rises in the forest, is little more than a stream, but as it grows larger and more important it evinces a great love of railways (or perhaps it is the other way round): it flows past the Bluebell Railway at Sheffield Park, once frequently flooded the Uckfield to Lewes line at Barcombe Mills, crosses under the coast line immediately east of Lewes and then keeps company with the Seaford branch all the way to Newhaven. In the nature of streams, and despite its diminutive size, the Ouse over millions of years had scooped out a great valley south of Balcombe and to bridge this Mocatta had Rastrick build for him a fine 1,475-feet-long viaduct, its 37 arches using no fewer than 11 million bricks. Helena Hall in her *Lindfield Past and Present*, published in 1960, claims that the Great Ouse Viaduct is 'the largest building in the world made only of bricks, for besides them there is only the little stone parapet'.

Eleven million sounds an astronomical number, but the railway engineers were used to dealing in such quantities — Mocatta and Rastrick needed 10 million bricks for the 400-yards-long viaduct which carried the Lewes line over the London Road at Brighton. The total cost of the Great Ouse viaduct at Balcombe was £38,500. It was surely one of the all-

The Great Ouse viaduct with the River Ouse, up which the 11 million bricks needed to construct the viaduct were shipped, in the foreground.

time bargains, for in its 150 years it has needed no major repair work, despite the vast increase in the number and weight of trains passing over since the early years of Queen Victoria's reign.

Looking down on to the winding stream, it is difficult to imagine that the Ouse was once a busy waterway up to this point. Before the days of macadamized surfaces, Sussex roads could be excruciatingly bad. In summer they were passable, though rutted and dusty, but in winter the Wealden clay turned to mud, carts, coaches, horses and people stuck fast and one simply did not attempt journeys of any length. As the eighteenth century drew to a close, more and more landowners and industrialists were prepared to invest large sums in building canals and making rivers navigable. Between 1796 and 1811, £25,000 was raised to build locks and weirs and to widen and straighten the Ouse where necessary so that boats could proceed upstream from Lewes as far as the parish of Cuckfield. Prominent amongst the backers were the Burrells, Sheffields and Abergavennys. There is a Burrell Arms opposite Haywards Heath station, no one who has ever visited the Bluebell Railway needs to be reminded of Sheffield Park and its station, whilst the Abergavennys had been Lords of the Manor since around 1450; a Brighton-built 'Pacific' tank would bear their name in the twentieth century.

For 50 years the Ouse was the principal carrier of goods from Cuckfield, Lindfield and district to Lewes and beyond. Then came the railway. For a couple of years the river was busier than ever bringing up the bricks, lime, French coping, stone and other building materials to the landing stage at Balcombe for Rastrick and his men. As late as 1847, £800 worth of business came up the Ouse beyond Lewes and local newspapers advertised the most convenient route for conveying goods between Newhaven and London as being along the 30 miles of the river to Balcombe and thence by train. But that was to be its swan song, for the opening of the Lewes to Newhaven branch was the death blow. Naviga-

Clayton Tunnel House.

tion ceased above Lindfield in 1861, and between there and Lewes seven years later.

Immediately south of Haywards Heath is a short tunnel of 249 yards. Once through this, there on the horizon is the great ridge of the South Downs. At Clayton, 44¾ miles from London Bridge, trains plunge into the longest tunnel on the line. Steaming through a tunnel in an open carriage must have been a both exhilarating and terrifying experience; just how terrifying we shall shortly see. Appreciative of this, the company built a gas works at Hassocks, north of the tunnel, which supplied jets which were placed at intervals along the tunnel roof to light the way; in addition, the brick lining was whitewashed. As with Balcombe Tunnel, there were some initial problems with water from the forest streams seeping through, but these were overcome and the tunnel was ready on time. The Brighton company was justly proud of Clayton Tunnel and at the southern portal two Normanesque turrets were erected, facing travellers from the London direction. Immediately behind the portals a tunnel-keeper's house was built, surely one of the most remarkable dwelling places in the land. It has been occupied ever since.

Clayton marks the summit of the line and from there it is

Brighton station as originally built before the carriage canopy was added and Queen Street was built up to lead directly into it (Brighton Library).

The Brighton Terminus of the London & Brighton Railway

Drawn by F.W.Woledge.

Eng by J.Newman.

Pub by C.Widnell, 2 S.t James S.t

downhill, through the 492-yards-long Patcham Tunnel and so to Brighton.

So distinguished and so well engineered a line deserved a handsome terminus, and Mocatta determined on the Italianate style. At that date most architecture in the town was, inevitably, Regency, and to this day it gives the character to much of Hove and many parts of Brighton. But by the mid nineteenth century the Regency style was dead and the Gothic revival was in full flood. Many architects were also turning to the Mediterranean for inspiration, and Palladian windows, Venetian arches, Florentine palazzios and the like became all the rage. Thomas Cubitt built Osborne House on the Isle of Wight for Queen Victoria in this style, although the real architect was Prince Albert, and it was very popular for hotels and apartments at both ends of the Brighton line. Kensington, Pimlico, and Belgravia sport many examples, whilst in Brighton the most notable is Palmeira Square, built between 1855 and 1870.

Brighton station was greatly admired. The *Brighton Herald* was 'amazed' at it, with its 'vast arching roof upheld by dazzling columns of cast-iron'. Built of pale yellow stone, the entrance was through nine portico arches. It faced Queen's Road, which led directly down to the sea, a mile away, although there was at first no direct link with it, the entrance opening on to the steeply sloping Trafalgar Street which led down to London Road and the Steine.

A present-day view of Brighton station at night.

EARLY DEVELOPMENTS

Through trains between London and Brighton began on Monday 20 September 1841. The Directors set off in three first class carriages and made a triumphal progress through Surrey and Sussex. Huge numbers of spectators came to watch, and Clayton Tunnel was especially illuminated. The ornamental facings were not quite finished but this did not affect the running of the trains. As the train approached its destination, the *Brighton Gazette* noted that it was 'applauded by many of the inhabitants of this town'. Afterwards a great feast and speech-making was held at the Old Ship Inn for 'upwards of 200 gentlemen'. (Whether this meant that no ladies were present or that those females who accompanied the gentlemen could not be called ladies, the report does not enlighten us.)

Prominently on its front page, the *Gazette* displayed the timetable. There were six up and six down through trains each

A contemporary print 'Waiting for the Train' published at the time of the opening of the Brighton railway (Brighton Library).

WAITING FOR THE TRAIN.

weekday, fewer on Sundays. The fastest, the 8.30 am up and the
4.45 pm down, ran non-stop in $1\frac{3}{4}$ hours ('No private carriages
or horses will be carried by the Express Train'). Slow trains took
$2\frac{1}{2}$ hours.

When public services began on Tuesday 21 September, the day
after the Directors' excursion, 'only a few passengers availed
themselves of the opportunity of making the first trip to town by
railway' owing to the miserable weather, 'a dense sea fog which
approached almost to rain'. (It is interesting to note that going to
London was already spoken of as 'going to town'.) However,
traffic soon picked up and the paper was able to announce that
'the building of a London terminus for the Brighton line,
altogether distinct from the Greenwich line . . . is proceeding
rapidly.'

At the opening, or within a short time of it, 17 intermediate
stations were in use. These were New Cross (later New Cross
Gate), Dartmouth Arms (later Forest Hill), Sydenham, Penge
(later Penge West), Anerley Bridge (later Anerley), Jolly Sailor
(later Norwood, later still Norwood Junction), Croydon (later
East Croydon), Godstone Road (later Purley), Stoat's Nest,
Merstham, Reigate (later Redhill), Horley, Three Bridges,
Balcombe, Haywards Heath, Burgess Hill, and Hassocks Gate
(later Hassocks). One is immediately struck by how many stations were to change their names. Others changed their locations
and almost always this was because the coming of the railway
brought great changes to the locality of each station. Development invariably followed, houses, commercial premises and occasionally industries appeared, and the original station often
proved inadequate for the increasing traffic or was found to be inconveniently sited; its location, instead of being merely a public
house or a crossing place on the road to somewhere else, became
a settlement in its own right.

Over the years other stations were built, and, unlike most main
lines, very few have ever closed and those that have closed have
usually been replaced or relocated. Indeed, those fortunate souls
living along the Brighton line have probably been better served in
terms of the number of stations and the frequency of trains, if not
always the quality, than anywhere else in the country.

South of New Cross, the still largely rural area was gradually
built up; Brockley station was opened in March 1871, whilst
Honor Oak Park appeared in April 1886. Within sight of East
Croydon, South Croydon opened in September 1865, and the
next station, Purley Oaks, dates from November 1899, and came
into existence when the main line south of South Croydon was
quadrupled. Coulsdon North also dated from this time, whilst

'W' Class 2–6–4T No 31925 in charge of a freight from the Oxted line heading northwards through South Croydon station, 9 July 1963 (J. Scrace).

Coulsdon South is somewhat older, having opened in October 1889. Earlswood was opened in 1868, Salfords was built as late as 1932, whilst the original Gatwick Airport was even newer, being opened as Tinsley Green in September 1935. The present Gatwick Airport station first saw the light of day as Gatwick Racecourse in 1891. Wivelsfield opened as Keymer Junction in 1886, changing to its present name ten years later. Finally the Brighton suburban station at Preston Park was opened as Preston in November 1869.

Godstone Road was closed as long ago as 1847 while Stoat's Nest disappeared in 1856. However, when the latter ceased business, the former re-opened under the name of Caterham Junction (later it would become Purley) and a new Stoat's Nest appeared from the ashes of the original in 1899. Twelve years later it was renamed Coulsdon and Smitham Downs, in early July 1923 it became Coulsdon West and finally, three weeks later, the compass was reconsulted and it was decided that the location was not west at all but north, and Coulsdon North it remained for the rest of its existence.

Not everyone welcomed the railway. There were those who always have and always will resist any change, whether it holds out potential for good or bad. Then there were those who had sound commercial reasons for fearing its coming, as well as those whose peace and quiet might be disrupted.

It is difficlt to know within which category the landowners of Cuckfield fitted—probably all three. To quote from a history of the town published in 1912, 'As with many another country town the conservatism of Cuckfield in the first half of the nineteenth century thrust aside the dangerous and new-fangled means of locomotion as an insult to those who lived on a great high road and profited thereby'.

When plans for the railway were announced, the landowners called a meeting at the Talbot Hotel and decided to buy up the land through which the railway hoped to pass. Cuckfield was the last staging post of the London to Brighton coaches and the amount of trade the Talbot Hotel did was enormous; it was no wonder it was happy to host such a meeting. The consequence was that the railway made a wide detour 'through a vast cutting

Below One of Maunsell's 'N' Class 2–6–0s heads a Battersea Yard to Brighton goods through Coulsdon North in March 1955.

Bottom Thirty years later, a twelve-coach Brighton to Victoria train passes the derelict and shortly to be demolished Coulsdon North, 27 May 1985.

Passengers at Haywards Heath station. In the background, Home Counties mock-Tudor houses.

in the heathland' which subsequently became Haywards Heath. Of course once the railway was working, the inevitable happened — within four years all the stage coaches had ceased to run. Cuckfield, once so important, became 'a rather decayed little country town', and the Talbot went out of business.

And what of Haywards Heath where in 1837 the railway had bought 'a strip of land'? Never had such excitement been seen since December 1642 when the Roundheads and Cavaliers had fought a pitched battle for an hour on the heath, resulting in some 300 casualties. The allegiance of the local landowners was evenly divided; the Parliamentarians won, the poor pressed men fled, the tide of war moved on and Haywards Heath disappeared back into obscurity after its one venture on to centre stage.

Haywards Heath was now the station for the ancient towns of Cuckfield and Lindfield and much of their trade came its way. Development was inevitable. In 1861 an application was made to the Commons Enclosure Commissioners to enclose the common and stop up some of the roads which passed across it. Some 137 acres were passed to the Lord of the Manor, the Earl of Abergavenny, and another 19 acres were sold off to others for

£2,090. The mind boggles at what 19 acres in the middle of Haywards Heath would fetch today!

The County Lunatic Asylum with its 800 inmates had moved to Haywards Heath in 1859. In 1865 the parish church of St Wilfreds — a rather handsome yellow stone and red-titled structure — was begun, a Local Government Board was set up in 1872, and by 1879 there was enough going on for the first directory for Cuckfield, Haywards Heath, Lindfield and Burgess Hill to be published. The Station Hotel acquired a croquet lawn, 30 gas lamps were erected in the streets of Haywards Heath, and just before the end of the century the cattle market became weekly and the LB&SCR laid on a special train which left for Brighton when the sales were over. Because the town was by then so well served by railway, not just by the main Brighton line, but by branches to Horsted Keynes and East Grinstead, and to Lewes, Newhaven and Eastbourne, the cattle market, alongside the railway on the up side north of the station, became the largest in central Sussex.

When the Urban District Council was formed in 1894 there were 2,452 inhabitants (929 of them patients and staff of the asylum). Included amongst the 1,553 outside the walls of the asylum were 20 policemen, 12 teachers and 415 schoolchildren. And all on account of the London to Brighton railway.

THE LONDON END

The story of the further development of the London terminus of the Brighton Railway is as complex as the station itself grew to be. The two original platforms at London Bridge were clearly not going to suffice for long, and even before the station was opened, extensions were planned and the land for them bought. The Croydon company had to pay the London and Greenwich $4\frac{1}{2}$d (2p) for every passenger it carried between Corbet's Lane and London Bridge. It resented this, strongly. Right was felt to be on the Croydon company's side — the Board of Trade said the levy was too high — but the Greenwich wouldn't budge. Goods traffic, which London Bridge was not designed to handle, was increasing, and thus in the 1842–3 session of Parliament a bill was presented for a new station to be built in the Old Kent Road near the Bricklayers Arms. This would be reached by a $1\frac{3}{4}$-miles-long line which left the Croydon line just before Corbet's Lane Junction. The promoters of the line and its new station were the Croydon and the South Eastern Railways, and thus we make the acquaintance of a railway company whose story is intimately entwined with that of the Brighton line.

The South Eastern Railway was incorporated on 21 June 1836, and was intended from the outset to be a trunk route linking London with England's ancient gateway to the Continent, Dover. It would have liked its own London terminus, and even before the Stockton and Darlington was opened, Thomas Telford had planned a railway route close to the Thames by way of Rochester and Faversham. But official insistence that London Bridge must suffice as the sole terminus for railways south of the river, and various impediments to the North Kent route, meant that the SER had entered into an agreement with the Croydon Railway to use its tracks. Originally the connection was to be made as an end-on junction at Croydon station, but in the event it was made at the Jolly Sailor (later Norwood Junction). It was the first of what would become a bewildering complex of junctions forming a triangle between Norwood, Selhurst and Croydon. It also marked the first move in the downgrading of the original Croydon station (later West Croydon) to secondary status compared with East Croydon, which would be opened on the new line to Brighton in 1841.

William Cubitt, the engineer of the Croydon Railway, was appointed Engineer-in-Chief of the SER, while Lewis Cubitt designed the impressive terminus at Bricklayers Arms, with its arches, porticos and clock tower. Apart from all the expected facilities for passengers, Bricklayers Arms greatly excelled London Bridge with a fine goods depot and a large space set aside for the sheep and cattle which were brought up from the country in great numbers to satisfy the needs of the ever-growing metropolis. Bricklayers Arms was billed as the 'Grand West End Terminus'. This it certainly was not, being no nearer to that part of central London than London Bridge, although it is true that the inn after which the station took its name was recognized as a stopping place for coaches 'to receive passengers from the west part of London', But this was not quite the same thing as being in the West End, and Bricklayers Arms' career as a passenger terminus, grand or otherwise, was to be a short one.

The station opened to passengers on 1 May 1844. Trains from Croydon ran every hour and omnibuses connected with the City and the West End. Fares were much lower than those to and from London Bridge, and this was the whole point of the exercise since there was no toll to pay to the London & Greenwich. After eight weeks, the Chairman of the Croydon company was able to report that receipts on the Bricklayers Arms line were treble those on the London Bridge one.

The Greenwich directors were aghast and quickly came to an agreement with the Croydon and South Eastern companies. The charges for the two latter using London Bridge were reduced so that the same fare applied to and from each terminus, and they were served by an equal number of trains. In less than a year, Croydon passenger trains ceased to use Bricklayers Arms.

There is no doubt that one of the principal reasons for the new station's construction was to persuade the Greenwich Railway to reduce its tolls, yet it surely cannot also have been intended that once this was achieved the grand and expensive facilities should be totally abandoned. But the directors of the Brighton company, as it then was, declared that the Bricklayers Arms branch was 'unproductive' and they gave it up, except for goods traffic. This latter was heavy, so there was no loss of revenue as far as the line and the freight side of the establishment was concerned. Nevertheless, the building of impressive passenger facilities which fell out of use within 12 months hardly seems businesslike.

By this time also, London Bridge station had grown considerably. As we have seen, a separate set of platforms had been built for the Croydon company to the north of the Greenwich facilities and a goods station beyond this. At first, Croydon and

Greenwich trains used the same two tracks to approach the station, so the fact that the Croydon trains came to Corbet's Lane Junction from the south but ended up north of the Greenwich tracks did not matter. But, when a Select Committee of the House of Commons recommended that additional approach lines should be built, it was only sensible that the Croydon trains should occupy both the southernmost tracks and the southern part of the station, and thus keep clear of the Greenwich trains. The four tracks were completed in May 1842 and the new station opened and the exchange made by the spring of 1844. No longer were the platforms uncovered, and London Bridge was becoming an impressive, extremely busy, if somewhat rambling, establishment.

William Cubitt was once more the engineer, and Henry Roberts the architect of the 1844 building. A man with a deep social conscience, Roberts was honorary architect to the Society for Improving the Conditions of the Labouring Classes which was founded by Lord Shaftesbury in the same year as the new London Bridge was opened.

It was a society for which there was a desparate need. A 'Report on the Sanitary Conditions of the Labouring Classes' published in 1842 revealed that over one-third of the population of London lived in slum conditions, the majority immediately east of the City alongside the banks of the river in Shadwell, Whitechapel, Rotherhithe, Deptford and district. This population had grown from something under a million when the century opened to close on two million 40 years later.

The railways both contributed to and alleviated the misery of the labouring classes. Elevated lines, such as that on the approach to London Bridge, were encouraged to avoid level crossings on heavily congested streets, and Parliament hoped that the arches might be used for schools and houses. By and large they were not, being chiefly occupied by the poorest types of tradesmen and derelicts, and rapidly becoming a symbol of the worst sort of city dwelling. Areas in the inner suburbs surrounded by railways, New Cross for example, declined in value. The people were crowded into tenements in an ever-decreasing space and slums were created. The Shaftesbury Standing Order of 1853, introduced following the recommendation of a committee headed by Lord Shaftesbury, required every proposed railway scheme to say how many working men and their families were likely to be evicted if its line was built. Re-housing in the locality by the railway companies was recommended, but this did not often happen. Other statutes required that specially low workmen's fares were available on early morning trains (many started work bet-

Urchins in the East End
(Author's collection).

ween 6 and 7 am). However, at this time most workers lived
within walking distance of their place of employment; in the
mid-1850s there were some 27,000 daily rail commuters, but
244,000 who travelled by omnibus or walked. It was only for
distances of upwards of six miles that the railways really came into their own.

One witness to the 1884 Royal Commission on Housing of the
Working Classes, when asked if he believed that a railway company had the right to exclude the lower classes from certain areas
in order to earn better dividends from better areas, replied, 'I do
indeed'. Just how great the dividends could be of owning land in
'better areas' when a railway arrived in their midst is shown by
what happened in Redhill and Reigate when the London,
Brighton & South Coast and the South Eastern railways were
built. In 1839, land in Redhill was worth £50 an acre; 30 years
later it was worth £700. In Reigate, rather more up-market, in
1839 an acre was worth £35, in 1867 £1,000.

The cost of land compulsorily bought for railways was based
on its value to the vendor, and compensation had to be paid. This
could include what the land might have been worth if it had been

built on, even if it wasn't. Thus, as soon as a Bill for a line was deposited in Parliament, the speculators rushed in and bought up as much as they could lay their hands on. In 1845, at a time when there were 2,234 miles of railway in existence in Great Britain and Ireland, Parliament authorized the construction of another 2,170 in that one year. An excess of enthusiasm, and often simple greed, led to money being promised which the investors did not possess, shares being resold at huge profits, and any jobbing journeyman who claimed to be an expert being taken on as an engineer.

Thus the Railway Mania came about. The boom broke in October 1847, bringing ruin to many, most notably George Hudson. Some of the lines which had been authorized were never built. Directors and others closely involved in a new railway scheme were in the best position to profit from the land boom for they were able to buy before the plans were made public and all and sundry rushed in. Not surprisingly, there were railway promoters and boards of directors who fiercely resisted attempts by Parliament and men with conscience to legislate, and it was claimed that concern for public interest discouraged investors coming forward to finance new schemes.

However, there were many who financed and built the railways who had a social conscience and Roberts, the architect of the 1844 rebuilding of London Bridge station, was a pioneer of decent housing for the working classes and wrote much on the subject. Gilbert Scott, architect of St Pancras, the most spectacular railway station in Britain, was a junior in Henry Roberts's office in the 1830s and later described him as 'a gentlemanly, religious, precise and quiet man'. Roberts retired to Italy in 1855 and died in Florence. Although his station was much admired for its 'handsome Italian palazzo style' and campanile, it did not last long for there was to be yet another rebuilding in 1851 which erased most of his work.

WHEELING AND DEALING

One of the most curious features of the Brighton company's main line was that quite a lot of it belonged to someone else. It was all the fault of Parliament and the government in power at the time of Queen Victoria's accession, headed by Lord Melbourne. Not that the noble lord himself had much to do with it, but the conservative-minded prediction that there would never be sufficient traffic to warrant more than one line south to Surrey, Kent and Sussex resulted in four companies owning parts of the first 21 miles of the Brighton main line between London Bridge and Redhill — or Earlswood as it was then called. The London & Greenwich owned the first section as far as Corbet's Lane, the London & Croydon took over to the Jolly Sailor, from there it was London & Brighton territory to Stoat's Nest, and the final bit was the South Eastern's.

In May 1842, South Eastern Railway trains began to run from London by way of Redhill to Tonbridge, by December they had reached Ashford, in June 1843 they were using a temporary terminus at Folkestone, and in December of that year, following the

Redhill station looking south, circa 1909. The trains on the right are SECR, that on the far right being in the charge of a Stirling 0–6–0, whilst an LB & SCR express is passing the signal box on the left (Lens of Sutton).

opening of the 100-feet-high viaduct spanning the northern part of the town, were at Folkestone proper. Finally, after a way had been blasted through and along the foot of the white cliffs, Dover was reached in February 1844. The section from Redhill to Ashford was remarkably straight, the 26 miles from Tonbridge through the Kent orchards and hop fields being without the slightest deviation, which made it, as it still is, the straightest piece of track in the British Isles.

Passengers at London Bridge now had the convenience of a choice from a whole variety of destinations along the Sussex and Kent coasts, and for a short while all was sweetness and harmony. One of the many Cubitts, Benjamin, had charge of designing the South Eastern Railway engines, and from March 1844 until January 1846 the locomotives of the Croydon, Brighton and South Eastern companies were under joint managership.

There are plenty of other examples in the early days of companies sharing a main-line approach to a London terminus — the Great Northern and the Midland into King's Cross (another Cubitt family enterprise); the Great Eastern and the London, Tilbury & Southend into Fenchurch Street; even the Great Western planned to share Euston with the LNWR only to change its mind at the last minute (hence the sharp right-hand turn at Old Oak Common). Whilst one central London terminus for all would have been a great convenience, it would have had to have grown to such proportions that it would have swallowed up much of the City of London and a good deal of the West End. Sheer heaven to railway buffs, but a bit of a blow to merchant bankers, admirers of Christopher Wren, and several thousand civil servants!

As it was, none of the north and west London sharing arrangements lasted for long, apart from a few minor workings, and it would have been as well if the Brighton and the South Eastern had also gone their own separate ways as soon as possible. But it would be over 20 years before what is now thought of as the South Eastern main line through Hither Green, Bromley, Polhill and Sevenoaks to Tonbridge was opened. Even then, many SER trains still used the original Croydon and Redhill route. Neither the Grouping nor electrification could totally wipe them out, and it wasn't until the early 1960s that the last survivors disappeared from the Southern Region timetable.

As traffic both to the Kent and Sussex coasts grew apace, so the problems of sharing the crowded tracks grew. The SER leased the London & Greenwich at the beginning of 1845. Then, on 27 July 1846, the London, Brighton & South Coast Railway came into existence when the Croydon and Brighton companies

amalgamated. This meant that there were now only two instead of four companies sharing the line from London Bridge to Redhill, but the rivalry merely intensified. At Redhill — then still known as Reigate — there was the ridiculous situation of three stations, all rather inconveniently placed. There were the two of the Brighton company, Merstham to the north of the junction and Reigate to the south, and the SER station, also called Reigate, round the curve beyond the junction. There was little attempt to organize the timetable in a manner which was convenient for passengers who wished to change from Brighton to South Eastern trains or vice versa.

However, in July 1848 common sense broke out and a complicated peace treaty was signed. The essence of it was that tolls would be abolished, each company would keep within its own territory, and SER trains would be limited in the number of LB&SCR stations they could stop at. In the next few years, further tracks were added north of Croydon which enabled SER and LB&SCR trains to be segregated, but south of Croydon delays and thus friction remained. Redhill was where most of the shenanigans occurred and it is generally alleged that it was all the fault of the SER signalmen who, either instructed from on high or on their own initiative, made life difficult for the Brighton company. There is, however, another school of thought which suggests that it was more the nature of the complications inherent in the layout than any malice aforethought. I incline to the latter theory myself, if only because a study of any period of world

Redhill looking north in 1972. A Class '47' is heading a stone train from the Western Region to the M23 road works at Gatwick whilst a Tonbridge to Reading Tadpole DEMU stands at the platform.

Redhill shed in 1969, after the end of steam but before its demolition. A LMR London area suburban EMU being used for braking tests and attached to a former GWR goods brake van stands in the shed whilst a Tonbridge-bound Tadpole DEMU heads eastwards along the original SER main line.

history ought to convince anyone that 99 per cent of all world-shattering events happen by accident and mismanagement rather than highly detailed planning.

A line with which the South Eastern Railway was deeply involved at the time of the agreement on sticking to territories not only took it west of any LB&SCR line but for good measure carried it beyond the LSWR too; it kept going until it reached the Great Western's main line, no doubt to the latter's considerable astonishment. This was the Reading, Guildford and Reigate Railway. Nominally independent, the Redhill to Dorking and Reading to Farnborough sections opened in July 1849, the complete line coming into use in October of that year. Not surprisingly, the LB&SCR was pretty cross, its lawyers rubbed their hands at the prospect of yet more business coming their way, and Parliament stipulated that traffic must start at the Reading end of the route, presumably as a gesture to persuade the Brighton company that a cross-country link was the main purpose of the line.

By 1852 the South Eastern Railway had bought the line outright and it immediately set about trying to steal as much traffic from the LSWR and the GWR as it could. Seeing that these latter had vastly shorter routes between London and anywhere the Reading–Redhill line served, they had little to worry about. The real value of the line would become apparent decades later when through trains from the GWR and beyond began to run over it on their way to the Kent and Sussex coasts.

Our chief interest in the line, however, is that it resulted in the junction with the Brighton and Tonbridge lines at Redhill which over the years has provided such a variety of traffic, some of it from far corners of the British railway system.

A new station was built at Redhill in April 1844, immediately north of the junction of the Tonbridge and Brighton lines. Tonbridge and Reading trains both came in on sharp curves subject to severe speed restrictions and through running without reversal from one line to the other has never been possible; had it been, there were periods when it would have proved immensely useful and much delay and confusion would have been avoided. Even when a new station was built, it did not assume its present name; this happened when the real Reigate, some two miles west along the Reading line, was opened in 1849.

The middle years of the nineteenth century was a period when lines connecting with the London and Brighton were being opened as rapidly as the money and the manpower could be found. Not all are relevant to our story but there are some of which we should certainly take note. One which to this day possesses a peculiarly rural air for a line wholly within the London suburbs is that from West Croydon to Wimbledon. Much of it was built along or close to the trackbed of the Surrey Iron Railway; opened as an independent line in October 1855, it was leased by the LB&SCR the following year. Single track for much of its length, it has so remained, despite being electrified in 1930. It has been threatened with closure from time to time but has survived along with an old-fashioned, almost Victorian air of faded gentility.

THE FIRST LOCOMOTIVES

A railway is probably most easily identified by its locomotives, and the London, Brighton & South Coast Railway possessed some of the most distinctive in the land. But not straight away. It wasn't until William Stroudley became Locomotive Superintendent in 1869 that engines of an individuality and quality began to be seen which would make the company famous.

In the beginning, the company got through three Superintendents in a little over six years. Statham was the first, followed in 1845 by Gray who was in turn succeeded by S. Kirtley in early 1847. His tenure of office was shortest of all, John Chester Craven taking over later that year. Craven was to be in charge for 22 years; but more of him later.

In the April 1903 issue of the *Railway Magazine*, the then Locomotive, Carriage and Wagon Superintendent of the LB&SCR, R. J. Billinton, was asked 'whether the company in its earlier days had any locomotive freaks or other curious or notorious engines?' (Possibly the interviewer had a premonition that he would one day be offered employment on *Sunday Sport* . . .) Nothing daunted, Billinton replied that the company had 'some very interesting locomotives' including a 'single' built by Bodmers of Manchester in 1845 which had two cylinders each containing two pistons working in opposite directions. Although we are not told how successful this curious arrangement was, Billinton remarks that the engine was put in charge of 'the first 5 pm train from Brighton to London', so it couldn't have been too bad. But the most interesting aspect of the story is a picture accompanying it. This shows the engine, No 292 *Seaford*, in immaculate condition with its tall, Bury-type 'haycock' firebox with a huge bellmouth safety valve atop, a cab a good deal more substantial than the Brighton normally fitted to its engines in the 1840s, and indeed 1850s, and painted in full Stroudley livery. All this means it must have survived well into the 1870s and have been rebuilt at least once. A lifespan of 25 years was far above the average for the time; No 292 may have been a one-off, but she was a distinctly long-lived one.

The well-known firm of Hackworth built twelve 2–2–2s to Gray's design in 1846–8 with a 'novel expansive valve gear', two of which were converted to Cramptons; a crank axle with no wheels was employed, the drive being by the trailing wheels which were connected by a coupling rod to the crank axle. Billinton tersely comments that, 'Needless to say, these engines proved far from satisfactory'. This was a bit hard of Billinton, for whilst the Brighton Cramptons were a failure, elsewhere, especially in France, they achieved considerable popularity. As late as 1890 a Paris, Lyons and Mediterranean Crampton achieved the world land speed record when it reached 89.5 mph, and a Paris-Strasbourg Railway Crampton is preserved in working order at the French National Railway Museum at Mulhouse in eastern France.

Billinton was kinder about the 'Jenny Linds', a rather different type of 'single' express engine. These were designed by David Joy and worked on a number of railways but, so it was claimed, 'were designed specially for the Brighton Railway'. Jenny Lind was a celebrated Swedish opera singer whose fame was at its height when the design appeared, hence its name.

According to that great authority on the Brighton, O. J. Morris, John Chester Craven, who had charge of locomotive affairs for 22 years, was 'a dour taciturn character'. Morris knew old railwaymen who had known Craven, and no doubt these comments are true. But Ben Webb speaks highly of his engineering ability. 'He was a very thoroughgoing, ingenious and versatile experimenter . . . and lived only for his job.'

Today Craven is chiefly remembered for the enormous variety of engines he produced. When he retired at the end of 1869, the company owned 233 engines, divided into no fewer than 72 different classes. This certainly was extraordinary and was in great

Four old Craven-designed outside-framed 0–6–0s; the leading one is No 468 (Brighton Libraries).

Craven 0–4–0T No 400 in Stroudley livery (Author's collection).

contrast to such railways as the Great Western and the London & North Western, or even the neighbouring London & South Western, where standardization was making considerable headway. In some respects, Craven's career paralleled that of Joseph Beattie on the LSWR. The latter took over at Nine Elms in 1850, three years after Craven became LB&SCR chief, and he died in office in 1871, within a year of Craven's retirement. Beattie produced only a small number of designs, but a great many engines. Best remembered are the 85 2–4–0 'well tanks' which once monopolized the suburban traffic out of Waterloo, many later migrating to the country. But whilst these were so long lived that three survived into British Railways days, and two, much rebuilt, have been preserved, no Craven engine was still at work when the twentieth century dawned, unless one counts a six-coupled goods engine, No 614, which lasted until July 1901 as a stationary boiler. Even so, this was 35 years old when broken up, which was pretty good going.

It has been suggested that the reason for the proliferation of designs in Craven's time was that this was the period when the LB&SCR network was being built up, and as each new line was opened so a new type of engine was constructed to work it. If this is so, it is still remarkable on two counts. No other railway pursued such a system to anything like the degree entered into with such enthusiasm on the Brighton. Secondly, there was nothing like the variation in the characteristics of the lines to justify it.

Some of the Craven engines were good and there were enginemen who remained loyal to them long after they had been superseded by Stroudley designs. But others were dreadful, certainly in their declining days even if they had possessed some virtues when new. In his latter years, Craven seems to have let things slip, and standards of maintenance fell badly. Michael Reynolds, the Brighton running shed superintendent in the years immediately after Craven's departure, describes a situation where the backlog of engines needing heavy repairs was constantly growing. 'Things were as bad as could well be.'

None the less the best of Craven's engines ran for many years and gave the company excellent service. Others were rebuilt by Stroudley and for a year or two after he had taken charge at Brighton he continued to produce Craven-designed engines, but with his own modifications. There were, for instance, eight double-framed express 2–4–0s. Stroudley never normally went in for double frames, or, indeed, 2–4–0s. Four were rebuilds of Craven singles, and all were given Stroudley boilers, cabs and other features. In this form they lasted for some 25 years.

Craven himself was not a popular figure. He lived on the premises, in rooms at Brighton station, which was certainly handy but can hardly have been ideal for his family. According to Morris, when the family moved out on Craven's retirement to Wellington Villa, 'it was regarded as a point of honour by every passing engineman either to spit in his shrubbery, or shake a cautious fist at his windows'.

A highly decorated Craven express 2–4–0, No 174 in 1869 (Author's collection).

RAILWAYMEN

And what of Brighton itself now it had its railway to London? The Queen paid her first visit following the railway's completion in February 1842. For a little while, the Pavilion, completed in all its oriental magnificence in 1822 by which time the Prince Regent had become George IV, would continue to be the seaside residence of the monarch, although Victoria's would be 'angel's visits, few and far between'. She arrived at the Chain Pier from a foreign tour in the autumn of 1843, her three children stayed in Brighton in 1844 and in February 1845 Victoria and Albert and their growing family, there now being four children, returned to the Royal Pavilion. However, on their drives around the town and walks along the promenade they were 'increasingly irritated by the attentions of the crowd, now swollen by carriage-loads of trippers transported by the new railway from London'. They returned to London by train, Albert with a streaming cold. By the end of the year, the vastly more secluded Osborne House on the Isle of Wight had been bought, Albert had set about redesigning it, and in August 1846 it was announced that the Royal Pavilion was to be sold. Never again, during the remaining 55 years of her reign, would Queen Victoria visit the resort and palace over which the Prince Regent had 'cried for joy'.

But if the Brighton of the railway age was not to royal tastes, it certainly suited others. The population, which in 1825 had been 24,000 had, by 1854, when the town acquired its first mayor, risen to almost 70,000. In 1852, the LB&SCR works turned out its first locomotive and the railway was one of the chief providers of employment.

Jobs on the railway were much sought after and the management could pick and choose its employees. Guards, policemen, switchmen and even porters had to be able to read, which in 1849 with universal primary education 20 years in the future would have sent a great many applicants away disappointed. It is interesting to look at the previous employment of a group of applicants around 1860: eight had been soldiers, seven agricultural labourers, seven general labourers, seven domestic servants and six shop assistants.

Many of those fortunate to find work with the LB&SCR in Brighton lived with their families in the terraces around the station. Those of the Anglican persuasion attended St Bartholomew's, a truly remarkable church down the hill from the station. A towering brick-built edifice, designed by a Brighton architect Edmund Scott (being born a Scott in Victorian times almost guaranteed a career in architecture!), it is four feet higher than Westminster Abbey, not counting spires or towers of which it possesses neither, and is said to be the tallest church in England. It utterly dwarfed the little terraces all around, and its vast bulk has been even more obvious since the 1970s when the surrounding terraces were demolished.

The houses built subsequent to the railway's arrival were generally of a higher quality than those put up for the working classes in the early years of the nineteenth century. These were often several storeys high, built around narrow courts where sunlight and fresh air seldom penetrated and into which open cesspools frequently overflowed; they quickly degenerated into fearful slums. Few associate slums with the affluent South Coast, but Brighton was ever the non-conformist. The scale was, of course, much greater in London and the industrial heartlands of South Wales, the Midlands and the North, but not even Liverpool, the unhealthiest town in the British Isles, could match the death rate from consumption in Brighton; in 1842, one-fifth of deaths in the town were from this disease. One of the chief causes

Brighton station in March 1988. In the distance is St Bartholmew's church, whilst the car park occupies the site of Brighton Works.

of this intolerable position was foul air. In seaside Brighton? Yes indeed. Dr N. P. Blaker, consulting surgeon to the Sussex County Hospital, discovered that fishermen's families tended to be rather healthier than others and concluded that this was caused partly by their fish diet and 'plenty of fresh air through cracks and crevices'. Some houses were so damp that water streamed down their walls and lichen luxuriated on them.

And yet a few streets away there were 'piles of buildings we suppose alone to be equalled at St Petersburg', to quote a guide book of the 1830s, whilst a few years later Arnold Bennett's Edwin Clayhanger would not be able to conceive 'what wealth can do when it organized itself for purposes of distraction'; he gazes in awe at the buildings on the promenade 'continually rising to the height of some gilt-lettered hotel, and at intervals sheer into the skies — six, eight, ten storeys — where a hotel, admittedly the grandest on any shore of ocean, sent terra-cotta chimneys to lose themselves amid the pearly clouds'.

But the other side of Brighton life was never far away, though there have always been those who have managed to avert their eyes from it. Suddenly a blind beggar comes tapping 'monotonously along . . . Edwin's heart seemed to be constricted. He thought of the ragged snarling touts who had fawned to him at the station, and of the creatures locked in the cellars whence

Brighton promenade, Kings Road, circa 1900 (Author's collection).

Horse carriages outside Brighton station circa 1890 (Brighton Libraries).

came beautiful odours of confectionery and soup through the gratings, and of the slatternly women who kept thrusting flowers under his nose, and the half-clad infants who skimmed before the wind yelling the names of newspapers.'

Unfortunate though all these latter were, they at least were able to earn a living, wretched though the reward might be. There were many others who could not even do this. In one particular week in 1899, 86 vagrants were recorded about the streets of Brighton whilst there were 1,541 living in the Workhouse. Another 2,240 were supported as 'outdoor poor'. Not surprisingly, drunkenness was rife amongst the poor — it was amongst the rich, too, but money and position ensured that authority turned a blind eye to it in that segment of society. Day-trippers added to the problem and in certain parts of the town the policemen would only venture out in pairs.

Between 1850 and 1870, the number of licensed premises in Brighton rose from 97 to 398. The LB&SCR, reasonably enough, did not approve of its employees drinking alcohol whilst on duty. They were banned from bringing it to work and from going into station refreshment rooms where alcohol was served. These, incidentally, in the early days when access to stations was open to all and no one had thought of platform tickets, got much of their business from passers-by and locals; it was only in the latter part of the nineteenth century that magistrates began to restrict access and hours of opening. There may be some connection between this and the number of dismissals of railwaymen for drunkenness, but certainly these fell drastically after 1860 and drinking on the job seems to have become a very minor nuisance.

Amongst the most fortunate railwaymen where those who lived in houses provided by the company. These were relatively few, around 10 per cent of the traffic grades employed throughout the system in 1861. Thirty-eight of these were station-masters, the rest ranging from guards and porters to three tunnelmen (presumably one of these was the chap perched high above the Clayton portal), one horse-keeper, four carters and a solitary labourer. The latter's weekly wage was 14 shillings and his rent was half a crown. The station-masters averaged 32/11d a week and paid 4/3d in rent, a lower percentage of rent against wages compared with the poor labourer.

Of course, if you lost your job you lost your home. A dismissed railwayman was given seven days' notice. In the period 1858–60, some 5 per cent of the 1,700 traffic grade employees lost their jobs, 13 for neglect, eight for insubordination and seven for drunkenness, these being the principal categories. Other offenders managed to get away with fines or reprimands. Some of their crimes sound familiar. There was the ticket collector who was 'cautioned for incivility', the telephone clerk 'fined for violently using his instrument' and the guard 'cautioned for taking a portmanteau beyond its destination'. Other offences involved enginemen, and amongst them were those of allowing a passenger to ride on an engine and not seeing that the tubes of an engine were cleaned out, while two engine cleaners were 'discharged for wilfully greasing the floor of the Engine Cleaners' Room'. Between August 1862 and December 1863, the company imposed 482 fines on its employees, an average of one fine per five employees per annum. This sounds a pretty high proportion, but does not seem to have been exceptional when compared with other companies.

A porter in 1871, of which there were 670 (not counting head porters, lamp porters, lad porters, etc) was paid 16/4d per week, a horse keeper 32/9d, a steam crane driver 25/4d, a ticket collector 18/9d, and a carriage cleaner 17/1d. The average annual income in Britain in 1860, taking into account that of Queen Victoria, a street sweeper and everyone in between, was £44, which means that the porter was marginally below the average, the carriage cleaner precisely equal to it an the ticket collector some £5 above.

A GREAT ENGINEER
EMERGES

The Brighton line has had its fair share of accidents. In the early days of railways, when one looks at the conditions which brought about an accident, one can only wonder that there were not many more. Just such was the Clayton Tunnel disaster. There is something peculiarly horrendous about a collision in the gloomy confines of a tunnel (the gas jets provided for the opening had long been extinguished). Three trains played their part in what was to be the worst disaster to date on the railways of Britain, although only two were actually involved in the collision.

Excursion trains had been a feature of the Brighton line from the beginning and by no means all of them headed towards the seaside, for a great many customers made use of the railway for a day out in London. On the morning of 25 August 1861, three trains were scheduled to leave Brighton within 25 minutes of each other. Today, such a headway would leave plenty of margin for safety, but 120 years ago the Brighton line, like most others, was worked on the time interval system, whereby the only regulation of trains following one another along the line was that there was supposed to be five minutes between each. Well, not quite the only regulation, for there were signal boxes at either end of Clayton Tunnel, with signals and handflags and a telegraph between them. Even so, these, as we shall see, were far from reliable. It seems unbelievable but the signalman in the South box regularly worked 24 hours a day. The directors of the LB&SCR hoped he would not do more than 18, but as the greedy man wanted a whole day off each week he elected to do 24.

The first train involved in the tragedy was an excursion from Portsmouth. Three minutes later — not five — another excursion originating at Brighton followed it up the main line, and four minutes after this the regular 8.30 am from Brighton departed. The Portsmouth train headed past Clayton South box and disappared into the tunnel, but did not work the signal which should have automatically showed danger after it had passed. By the time the South box signalman had telegraphed the North box, the second excursion train was approaching and had passed the signal which should have showed danger but didn't. The signalman rushed to the window frantically waving a red flag as the engine steamed past into the tunnel. He telegraphed again to the box on the far side of the tunnel and received the reply 'Tunnel clear'. He assumed that this referred to the second train. But it didn't — it meant the first. The third train was now coming up fast and the South box man, mistakenly assuming that both the Portsmouth and Brighton excursions were safely on their way, let it through.

It would have been better if he had not waved his red flag at the second train, or if the driver and firemen had not seen it. But he did and they had. The feeble brakes of the day (there were 17 well-filled four-wheel carriages behind the engine) were applied and the train slowly came to a halt deep in the tunnel. The driver started to set back in order to find out from the South box signalman what was wrong. As he did so, the third train thundered into his rear; 21 people died and 176 were badly injured.

An accident of such magnitude caused widespread alarm and the Board of Trade inquiry laid about the Brighton company with devastating invective. The LB&SCR method of operation was slack and inefficient on almost every count, and the report recommended that the absolute block system using electric telegraph instruments should be introduced immediately. It was perhaps unfortunate that the South Eastern Railway, which had pioneered this system between Merstham and Dover early in 1846, was cited as the paragon to be copied. L. T. C. Rolt, in quoting the reply the LB&SCR diretors sent to the Board of Trade, the gist of which was that too many signals took away the driver's initiative and made him more irresponsible, remarks 'we seem to hear no forgotten secretary but the cold, ghostly voice of John Chester Craven, that most formidable martinet among locomotive superintendents'.

The Brighton directors had to swallow their pride and the block system was installed experimentally between Brighton and Hassock's Gate (the latter was so called on account of it being the gateway to the Downs for the many walkers who took the train thus far). Of course, there could be no turning back once the system was working and had proved itself, and it eventually became universal. Indeed, great credit must be given the company, for interlocking — that is the interlocked operation of both signals and pointwork — was introduced in the early 1860s and was universal over the entire system by 1880, something no other company could claim at that date. Before this, as we have seen, the first recorded signal box, or 'lighthouse' as it was known, was operating at Corbet's Lane Junction in 1839, and a further pioneering effort was the installation of a semi-interlocking system at Bricklayer's Arms early in 1844.

A man who ought to be very nearly as well known as George Stephenson is John Saxby. His contribution to railway safety was unique and it is to the Brighton company's everlasting honour that he was an employee of theirs and did all his pioneer work whilst with them. In *The Signal Box*, compiled by the Signalling Study Group, the conclusion to the report on the Clayton Tunnel accident is quoted: 'In thus condemning the arrangements of the

John Saxby

Brighton Company . . . I am happy to add . . . that I have frequently had occasion to hold forth the convenient huts and stages that they have erected for the accommodation of their men, and the precautions in connecting the points and signals together, according to their foreman's patent . . . as an example to other companies.' That foreman was Saxby, and the first of his 'precautions in connecting the points and signals together' was patented and operating at Norwood Junction and Lewes Junction in April 1857.

John Saxby was born in Brighton on 17 August 1821, the son of John Saxby, a milkman, and his wife Elizabeth, who lived in Oxford Street, and was baptised in Brighton Parish Church on 23 September. In 1840, at the age of 19, he joined the London & Brighton Railway as a carpenter, and it is typical of railway technology in its very early days that a man with such a background would, through common sense, acute observation, and an innate understanding of engineering, become the key figure in the development of signalling. By the age of 25, Saxby was a foreman at Brighton Works and a year later he set up his own firm, although still employed by the Brighton company, in a building 'at or in the neighbourhood of Haywards Heath', possibly near Keymer Junction. It was rented from the company and Saxby was backed in his venture by the Superintendent of the Goods Department. By April 1862, Saxby was doing sufficiently well to give up his post on the LB&SCR. In his letter of resignation to Craven he writes that he is 'no longer able to give proper attention to his work as a foreman under his orders'.

This, however, was far from the end of Saxby's connections with the London, Brighton & South Coast Railway, for his firm was to provide its signalling requirements almost exclusively down to the end of the century. The Signalling Study Group lists the first 39 Saxby installations, and all but four controlled LB&SCR lines or lines over which LB&SCR trains regularly worked.

Saxby's boxes were built high up, naturally enough so that the signalman had a good view of approaching trains, and the signals often stuck out from the roof. They must have been draughty, rickety affairs, but were nevertheless a vast improvement on the open platforms which had gone before. At first the mechanical equipment below the floor of the box was left exposed, but it clearly made sense to enclose it and this development came about in 1863. A little later all new signals were fixed to posts independent of the box and thus the traditional signal box, still familiar in many parts of our railway system and throughout the world, was born.

Far left *An early Saxby signal box and signals at Brighton* (Author's collection).

Left *Worthing, a later Saxby signal box still in use in the autumn of 1988.*

EAST MEETS WEST

No one doubts that the industrial revolution vastly altered the map of many parts of Britain, raising up in South Wales, the Midlands, Lancashire, Yorkshire, the North-east Coast and the lowlands of Scotland places which previously had been of little or no consequence into great metropoli. And so it was in the south where fishing villages or totally empty tracts of beach and heathland found themselves transformed into pleasure resorts while at the same time once important inland market towns stagnated and declined; and the one common factor in all these changes was the railway. The railway helped Brighton become the greatest resort, certainly on the south coast, and it is around this rise that our story is woven. But Brighton did not, of course, rise in isolation, and we cannot ignore how the railway, and Brighton's pre-eminence, changed so much of Sussex.

Even before the main line between London and Brighton was in operation, thoughts had turned to extensions both east and west. A proposal for an independent line from Brighton to Lewes, for centuries the most important town in East Sussex, was sanc-

A 4COR EMU passing the junction with the Kemp Town branch on a Brighton-Hastings stopping service, June 1970.

tioned as early as 1837. Construction did not begin until the 1840s and by the time it was opened in June 1846 it was part of the LB&SCR. Just over a year later, in October 1847, a direct route was opened from London to Lewes. This branched off the Brighton main line at Keymer Junction, Wivelsfield. The curve taking the Lewes line away from the Brighton one was a steeply angled one of 14 chains radius, and not only did it mean that Eastbourne, Hastings and Newhaven expresses had to come almost to a halt, but also that their slow negotiation of the junction could cause delay to trains heading to or from Brighton. As long ago as 1879, the LB&SCR obtained powers to solve the problem with a flyover, but unfortunately it had second thoughts and decided it couldn't afford it. Later, plans were drawn up for quadrupling the main line right through to Brighton and these would have incorporated a revised layout at Keymer Junction, but again they came to nothing and the problem remains to this day.

On 27 June 1846, 19 days after the Brighton to Lewes line opened, it was extended along the coast through Polegate to Bulverhythe, on the outskirts of Hastings. Four years later, in February 1851, Hastings proper was reached, simultaneously with the arrival of the South Eastern Railway from the east at Ashford. You will not be surprised to learn that acrimony instantly broke out. But since Hastings is outside our brief, and also not wanting to upset those of a nervous disposition, any mention

of the horrid details — cutting off of gas supplies, injunctions and the like — will be judiciously avoided.

Hastings had been a resort of sorts ever since William of Normandy paddled there in 1066, but Eastbourne, in many respects Brighton's great rival and a town which one day would be able to boast more hotels and boarding-houses than anywhere else in Sussex, had to wait until four of George III's children visited it in 1780 before its star began to rise. Much of the land on which the town stands belonged to the Devonshire family, and in 1847 the Duke had a plan drawn up for the town's development. Two years later, the LB&SCR opened a branch from Polegate, and in the subsequent 50 years the population rose from 3,453 to over 53,000. At the same time, May 1849, another branch was opened from Polegate northwards to the market town of Hailsham. Eastbourne would increasingly overshadow Hailsham, and although a line would link it with Eridge, Oxted and Tunbridge Wells in 1880 and thus enable through trains from London to Eastbourne to take this route, it was never a serious rival to the Lewes line. Hailsham remained a pleasant little town to live in, even if most of its inhabitants looked to Eastbourne for entertainment; ironically, it lost its railway in 1969 just as it was entering a period of expansion.

Nearer to Brighton, a line which was to provide one of the route's most glamorous services opened in December 1847. This was the six-mile branch from Southerham Junction, east of Lewes, to Newhaven. Brighton was now connected to the county's two busiest harbours — and great rivals — Shoreham to the west, Newhaven to the east. Shoreham regarded the other very much as an upstart having only come into existence in the sixteenth century when the River Ouse changed course and deserted its previous mouth at Seaford.

Newhaven suffered from the silting up of its harbour mouth and to help cure this the Harbour Master at the time of the railway's arrival, William Stevens, had a groyne erected which doubled the depth of the water. This was only the beginning, for by the end of the nineteenth century the LB&SCR-owned Newhaven Harbour Company had spent close on £½ million on improvements. A Newhaven to Dieppe packet service had been running since 1825, operated by the General Steam Navigation Company, and, with the opening of the Shoreham branch, steamers began to operate between there and both Dieppe and Le Havre.

The Brighton and Continental Steam Packet Company was set up in 1847, largely with LB&SCR money, and it was originally intended that the steamers would operate from the Chain Pier,

TSS Brighton, *built on the Clyde by Dennys in 1903, and the first turbine steamer on the route, at Newhaven shortly after entering service* (Author's collection).

Brighton. Not surprisingly, this proved to be too exposed, so the company transferred its activities to Newhaven. Enter once again, stage left, the villainous South Eastern Railway.

Any cross-Channel services from Sussex ports were seen as a threat to those from Dover and Folkestone, in which the SER had a great interest. The SER perused the small print of every relevant Act of Parliament, and with a triumphant yelp discovered that the Brighton company had broken the law in investing in a shipping company, and took it to court. The LB&SCR was found guilty, fined, and had to give up its three ships (these were called, no doubt after many sleepless nights on behalf of whoever in the company had the job of naming its assets, *Brighton, Newhaven*, and *Dieppe*). The Newhaven–Dieppe route was contracted out until 1867, by which time the LB&SCR and the Western Railway of France had obtained powers to operate their own ships.

Amongst the improvements put in hand by the LB&SCR and its subsidiary, the Newhaven Harbour Company, created in 1878, was a new bridge for both road and rail traffic, which meant that rails ran down both sides of the quay, and a splendid hotel, the London and Paris.

In June 1864, the Newhaven branch was extended to Seaford, once a member of the Cinque Ports but a resort which never really developed, not least on account of the ferocious seas which sweep along its promenade and throw waves over the roof of its highest, five-storey, hotel.

Just as ambitions for extensions along the coast eastwards from Brighton had been entertained by many, so they had for heading off into the distant west. Trains began to work between Brighton and Worthing in November 1845, and were soon

reaching out further. Sussex's only cathedral town, Chichester, was connected by rail in June 1846; Havant, just across the Hampshire border, was first served by LB&SCR trains in March 1847; and finally the great naval town of Portsmouth was reached in June 1847.

Extending more than a certain distance along the coast from Brighton and the LB&SCR was certain to get a bloody nose. It had happened with the South Eastern Railway at Hastings and it happened with the London & South Western at Portsmouth, or, to be precise, Havant. Having enjoyed a monopoly for 11 years, the LB&SCR wasn't at all happy when the LSWR's direct line from Waterloo and Guildford reached Havant in December 1858. Fortunately we can once again pass over the horrid goings-on which resulted and which, as always, had to be solved by recourse to law.

Two resorts which the west coast line missed out were Littlehampton and Bognor, so branches to them had to be opened. The former was a port rather than a resort, but once the railway had arrived, in January 1887, the holidaymakers began to pour in. Bognor, which later acquired the suffix Regis on account of visits by King George V, got its railway in June 1864.

Any train bound for points west of Brighton had to travel the length of the main line, stop in the station and then reverse out of it and continue on its way with fresh motive power. Important though Brighton was, this was somewhat inconvenient. A through route to points east had existed since 1847, and the need for one to points west was obvious; the detour by way of Brighton certainly did nothing to help the Brighton company compete with the LSWR for the Portsmouth traffic. So, bit by bit, a route branching off the main line at Three Bridges, known as the Mid-Sussex line, was constructed. It got as far as Horsham in February 1848, reached Petworth in October 1859, and finally connected with the coast line at Arundel Junction in August 1863. Meanwhile, in Surrey, an alternative route out of London by way of Sutton, Epsom, Leatherhead and Dorking was being completed and when the final section from Dorking to Horsham came into use in May 1867, not only could the LB&SCR compete on serious terms with the LSWR for the Portsmouth traffic, but also a great deal of the pressure on the Brighton main line was relieved.

In September 1861, Shoreham was given an independent route to London when the line through Steyning to Horsham was opened; although very much a branch line, as the junction with the main coast line faced Brighton, it provided a realistic relief route between Brighton and London should it ever be so needed.

Left Hove station in April 1988. On the left, a Class '33' has just arrived with the 05.50 from Exeter St Davids whilst in the right foreground a West Worthing to Brighton EMU is about to depart.

Inset *One of the last active Stroudley 'D1' 0-4-2Ts, No 2252, at Southwater on 1 April 1950 with a Steyning branch Horsham to Brighton train* (Lens of Sutton).

CRYSTAL PALACE AND VICTORIA

Norwood gets its name from North Wood. At the dawning of the railway era, the remnants of this once large forest covering the slopes of the Downs where the boroughs of Lambeth, Croydon, Camberwell and Battersea met had all but gone, the great oaks cut down to supply the charcoal for the Croydon colliers. Right at its heart, on the 379-feet-high summit, stood the Vicar's Oak, 'an immense tree of great age'. It disappeared sometime after 1825, not very long before the Crystal Palace was erected on the site. It was the transfer of Paxton's remarkable structure from Hyde Park, after the Great Exhibition of 1851 had finished, to the outer southern suburbs of Norwood Heights which prompted the latter's growth and transformation into one of London's most sought-after residential districts.

The air up there was clean and bracing. In many respects it was the south London equivalent of Hampstead and Highgate. It even

The Crystal Palace as seen from the LB & SCR's Low Level station, circa 1905 (Author's collection).

had its own cemetery, like Highgate, where, in the fullness of time, the rich and successful owners of the ornate villas built on the wooded slopes were laid to rest. These included William Cubitt, Engineer of the Croydon Railway, Spurgeon, the famous Baptist preacher — there is a Spurgeon's tabernacle atop the bridge under which trains approach West Croydon station — Mrs Beeton, who was only 29 when she died, Jeremiah Colman, the mustard man, Henry Tate, the sugar man, and many others. Charles Dickens had David Copperfield and his first wife, Dora, set up house in Norwood.

The LB&SCR had long desired a West End terminus. Its first attempt, back in the days of the London and Croydon Railway, had been Bricklayers Arms. But now, with the arrival of the Crystal Palace on the Norwood heights, it seized with enthusiasm the opportunity both to tap the lucrative traffic this would generate and to reach the City of Westminster, not least because a number of directors of the Crystal Palace held similar positions on the LB&SCR. The first step was accomplished on 10 June 1854 when a station was opened in the south-west corner of the Palace grounds, not far from the life-size stone dinosaurs, and on the day that the Crystal Palace itself reopened in its new home.

Paxton's superb structure was to be the touchstone for railway termini the world over, from Milan to Victoria (the eastern side that is). Joseph Paxton himself had a villa called 'Rockhills' built for himself on the Norwood Heights so he could superintend the re-erection of his Palace. It stood above the tunnel through which trains approach the High Level station and he remained there until his death in 1865.

The style of Crystal Palace station as it finally appeared in the late 1870s after rebuilding and extending by Frederick Dale Banister and Whitney Mannering owed something to the French influence and echoed that of the Grosvenor Hotel built subsequently at Victoria in 1860–1. It was at the end of a branch which came up the hill from the main line at Sydenham, which meant that the Palace now had a direct rail link with central London, albeit the City rather than the West End. But this was just the beginning.

A third partner in the enterprise to open a West London terminus now emerged. This was the West End of London and Crystal Palace Railway, which proposed to connect with the LB&SCR at Crystal Palace and build a line through Wandsworth to Clapham Junction whence it would connect with the London & South Western. The West End of London and Crystal Palace would not itself operate trains but would allow the LB&SCR to pass over its tracks and thence to Waterloo. However, the LSWR decided it had insufficient capacity and the LB&SCR was not too upset for Waterloo wasn't really the West End. So instead, the LB&SCR put up £450,000 in 1858 towards yet another company, the Victoria Station and Pimlico Railway.

The Crystal Palace line duly reached Wandsworth, or Wandsworth Common as the station was shortly renamed, in December 1856, and, continuing through Clapham Junction, reached the south bank of the Thames at Battersea Pier in 1858. There, across the muddy water, on land owned by the Duke of Westminster, were the lock gates of the Grosvenor canal. A small section of the canal was retained and is in use to this day for barges which take away London's refuse, but upon the rest the

The handsome and recently restored facade of Battersea Park station, February 1988.

Victoria Station and Pimlico Railway laid its tracks, the station itself being built on the site of the canal basin. The Thames was spanned by the Grosvenor Bridge, down river from Chelsea Bridge and the open spaces of Battersea Park. It possessed four spans and was sufficiently high to permit the many craft which worked the river to pass safely beneath. On 1 October 1860, trains began to pass regularly over the bridge and the London, Brighton & South Coast Railway had at last attained its West End terminus. However, it didn't actually own it.

Back in the formative days of London's railways, practically everyone attempted to run services into everyone else's stations, partly in order to make connections, but partly to cream off other people's traffic. The GNR, the Midland, the LNWR and the GWR all ran in and out of Victoria, and the latter even had the nerve to put on a Paddington to Brighton service. There was also a Victoria to Birmingham through train. Not only this, but the GWR was part owner of Victoria.

Top *The ornate Victorian ironwork at Battersea Park station contrasts with the Gatwick Express air-conditioned stock speeding past (February 1988).*

Above *Grosvenor Bridge in the spring of 1988. Prominent to the left of the bridge is the handsome pump house whilst in the distance above the barges is the tower of Westminister Cathedral.*

Class '25' D7662 arriving at
Selhurst Yard with a
transfer freight from the
LMR, April 1973.

All these companies got in on the Victoria act by way of that immensely useful cross-London link, the West London Extension Railway, which passed through Kensington and crossed the Thames beside the house-boats, so beloved of film-makers in later days, between Chelsea and Fulham and Battersea stations. The Great Western, being a part owner of Victoria, installed mixed gauge tracks. Broad gauge trains did run into Victoria, however briefly, although there seems to be no photographic record of this. Not only were there suburban services to Ealing, Southall and Windsor, but Thomas B. Peacock in his *Great Western London Suburban Services* also records that a Bristol to Paddington express slipped a carriage at West London Junction for Kensington and Victoria. GWR services in and out of Victoria lasted for a surprisingly long time; they came to an end only during the First World War.

Even then, the GWR retained its financial interest in Victoria. This survived the Grouping and was not finally given up until 1932. None of the other connections was as successful, and all in the end succumbed to the competition of the underground and tube lines. Perhaps it was the fact that the only below surface link between Victoria and Paddington involved circumnavigating half of the Inner Circle line which kept the surface link going for so long. Parcels services and suchlike were a different matter, and they went on for many years, which is why the LMS, like the GWR, was financially involved in Victoria station after 1923. The LB&SCR tried to become sole owner in 1860 but failed, and it was only with the passing of the Railway Act in 1921 that its successor, the Southern Railway, legalized a position which probably almost all users of the station had always assumed existed. Certainly this was the impression created by the *Illustrated London News* in October 1860 which informed its readers that the station was seved only by the London & Brighton company; it did, however, suppose that 'other lines will no doubt speedily seek running powers'. They did indeed.

Not only this, but pretty soon there were two Victorias, side by side. Two months after Brighton trains began to use Victoria, another company serving the south of England started operations. This was not the Brighton's old partner/protagonist, the South Eastern Railway, but the latter's sworn enemy, the London, Chatham & Dover. As its title suggests, it provided a rival route to the Channel ports and the Kent coast. In the early days, the SER had a connection with the LC&DR at Strood, and had always assumed that the Chatham company would pass on its trains there so that the SER would take them thence to London. It therefore got a terrible shock, one from which it never quite recovered, when it discovered, horror of horrors, that the Chatham company had made arrangements to find its own way to London to the West End terminus at Victoria. The SER could do nothing to stop this, and the two companies entered into a murderous fight for Continental traffic which very nearly bankrupted them both and eventually brought about a forced marriage, the South Eastern and Chatham Joint Committee, in January 1899.

As it happened, the existence of a number of routes between London and the Channel ports proved to be most convenient, particularly in this century as the traffic has grown heavier and heavier. The last time I travelled to France we took the old Chatham route out of Victoria by way of Brixton and Herne Hill, switched to the former South Eastern line at Bickley to continue through Tonbridge and Ashford to Folkestone; we came back on former SER metals as far as Ashford, branching there to the LC&DR-built line through Maidstone for the rest of the way home.

One may look down from a London Bridge-bound train on the Brighton line just north of Penge West and watch a Victoria-

The forecourt of Victoria station in 1954 with the great bulk of the Grosvenor Hotel on the left looming over the bus station.

bound train on the former Chatham line diving underneath into the 2,200-yards-long tunnel. Originally Chatham trains used LB&SCR tracks from Bromley Junction, just north of Norwood Junction, and passed through Crystal Palace on their way to Victoria, but their own station at Victoria was opened in August 1862, and just under a year later, with the completion of Penge Tunnel, the direct route by way of Herne Hill and Brixton came into use.

The station took its name from Victoria Street, which linked Westminster Abbey and Pugin's brand new Houses of Parliament with Belgravia, and had been opened in 1851. The area around Victoria was, by the middle of the century, taking on a new aspect. Sir Thomas Cubitt had laid out the elegant terraces and squares of Belgravia. It was also the era of the department store, patronized by the affluent middle class, and Victoria Street could boast the Army and Navy Stores, a hundred yards away from Caxton Hall. The Victoria Palace theatre was opposite, and the Roman Catholic Westminster Cathedral, St James's Park and Buckingham Palace were all within a very few minutes' walk. London was expanding westwards and the Brighton company's West End terminus proved to be ideally placed. Gradually, over the years, it would supersede London Bridge as the principal departure point for the Sussex coast.

The Illustrated London News noted that the station, 'between the Vauxhall and Belgrave Roads', opened for public and excursion traffic without any special ceremony. 'The doors were thrown open, passengers took their tickets and the trains started as though the line had been in working order for years.' Although not quite finished, it would be the largest London terminus, albeit 'quite an ordinary one', according to the *Railway Magazine*. It grew quite quickly until it possessed nine platforms, but it was a gloomy old place. The Chatham station with its fine, Crystal Palace-inspired arched roof was much better. Quite the best bit on the Brighton site was the Grosvenor Hotel which sat at the north-west corner. It was one of the first buildings in London to employ what would become the very popular Italianate-cum-French pavilion roof style. It was the creation of J. T. Knowles, who did similar work around Clapham Common. Honey-coloured Bath stone was used, although it didn't take very long for the fume-laden Victorian atmosphere to render the honey but a faint memory.

Victoria station, the South Eastern side, in October 1986.

The Oxted line and Others

It is now time to consider a group of lines which not only provided various altenative routes between London and Brighton but in a rather remarkable way have, throughout the twentieth century, provided an everyday, working picture of the main Brighton line as it used to be at least one or, increasingly as the century has progressed, several generations back. This 'time warp' situation has become deliberate since the creation of the Bluebell Railway in 1960 (the first complete standard gauge preserved railway in the United Kingdom), but the Oxted line and its various branches and extensions had been providing a home for elderly locomotives and carriages long before that.

One of the original suggestions in 1839 for the route of the South Eastern Railway's main line to Dover had been by way of Oxted and Edenbridge, but in the event it was not until 1884 that the Brighton and the South Eastern companies opened a joint line from a junction with the Brighton line at South Croydon to Oxted. It was a most picturesque line, passing through some of the finest downland scenery Surrey had to offer, and for that reason was expensive to build. The gradient for the first six miles averaged 1 in 100 and included the 836 yards of Riddlesdown tunnel and a spectacular leap over the chalk pits at Whyteleafe alongside the London to Eastbourne road on the opposite side of the valley from the Purley to Caterham branch. High in the densely wooded slopes of the North Downs at Woldingham it reached its summit and then plunged down almost as steeply as it had ascended through the 2,266 yards of Oxted tunnel, jointly with Clayton the longest on the LB&SCR, and so arrived at Oxted, 9 miles from South Croydon.

Beyond Oxted, in the relatively level weald between the North Downs and the Ashdown Forest, a spur took SER trains up to join the Redhill to Tonbridge lines whilst LB&SCR trains continued southwards to East Grinstead. Here a station had been opened at the end of a single track branch from Three Bridges in July 1855. In October 1866, this station was replaced when another was opened on the extension of the line to Tunbridge

Wells. This latter was already served by the SER, so the old rivals were competing once again. Each had its own station, the LB&SCR's Tunbridge Wells West being a most imposing edifice at the bottom of the common just round the corner from the Pantiles and the spring which had brought the spa town into existence.

Meanwhile, down on the Sussex coast, the Brighton to Lewes line had in October 1858 been extended north-eastwards to the market town of Uckfield. Two years after the Three Bridges to East Grinstead line was extended to Tunbridge Wells, in August 1868, the Brighton, Lewes and Uckfield line also reached the spa town and thus one more route between London and Brighton — albeit one which for the time being necessitated reversal at Tunbridge Wells — came into existence. There would be more yet.

But let us return to the Oxted route. At this point, a calculator, compass, detailed OS map and cold compress are recommended, for the plot thickens. When the line from Croydon and Oxted reached East Grinstead in March 1884, it did not turn into the existing station served by the Three Bridges to Tunbridge Wells line but passed under it to a second station. It did, however, throw up a spur to the upper, or High Level, station. Meanwhile, the Low Level station turned out not to be a terminus but merely a stop on yet another route to Brighton, for in August 1882 a line

Brighton-built Standard 2–6–4T No 80084 leaving Riddlesdown Tunnel with a London Bridge to Tunbridge Wells West train returning from the rush hour, hence the two high-capacity former SECR non-corridors next to the engine. No 80084 had recently been transferred from Bletchley shed on the London Midland Region, which would explain its grubby appearance; Stewarts Lane, Tunbridge Wells and Brighton members of the class were generally kept commendably clean. 7 July 1961.

had been opened from just north of Lewes on the Uckfield line, by way of Sheffield Park and Horsted Keynes to East Grinstead. Originally, trains for the Uckfield line had left Lewes on the main Keymer Junction line and headed north-west in the London direction before branching off, but in October 1868 this was changed and a new junction was provided immediately to the east of Lewes station so that trains could run right through from Uckfield and beyond to Brighton without reversal. Now that the East Grinstead line was open, it meant that trains between London and Brighton could take this route.

Much of this network of lines came about whilst the LB&SCR was locked in a fierce battle with the SER to keep it out of its two most prosperous sources of income on the Sussex coast, Brighton and Eastbourne. In 1864, the London, Chatham & Dover, and then again in 1866 the LC & DR jointly with the SER, had put bills before Parliament for London to Brighton railways. The SER had also, in 1864, came up with a London to Eastbourne scheme. The LB&SCR was both enraged and worried, and counteracted by starting work on a direct line to Eastbourne, called the Ouse Valley Railway, which would leave the London to Brighton line at Balcombe and head through Uckfield and Hailsham. It also got permission to extend this on to St Leonards and to build the Surrey & Sussex Junction Railway which would

Former LB & SCR 'E4' Class 0–6–2 T No 473 Birch Grove and former SECR 'P' Class 0–6–0 T No 27 at Sheffield Park in May 1969.

run from Croydon to Oxted and Tunbridge Wells. Construction had just begun on the Ouse Valley and the Surrey and Sussex Junction lines when, in 1866, a financial crisis hit the country. The government of Lord Russell, with Gladstone as his Chancellor of the Exchequer, was brought down and the LB&SCR was one of many railway companies badly affected.

Disraeli became the new Chancellor and the LB&SCR gradually recovered; with a nicely judged sense of political balance, the company named its most famous express passenger locomotive, 'B1' Class No 214, after Gladstone and one of its illustrious brothers, No 218, became *Beaconsfield*, the title Disraeli later assumed. As H. J. Campbell Cornwell records in his *William Stroudley, Craftsman of Steam*, during the 1880s No 218 regularly worked the 8.45 am express from Brighton each 19 April, as it was used by members of the Primrose League, a Conservative party organisation, attending the Annual National Reunion in London that day. The locomotive bore a wreath on its smokebox door on 19 April 1881, Lord Beaconsfield having just died.

One of the consequences of the financial crash was the cessation of the work on the Ouse Valley and the Surrey & Sussex Junction railways. As these had both been intended to thwart the SER, the LB&SCR was quite happy to leave them where they lay,

A former SECR engine in charge of two LSWR-built carriages on Brighton metals. 'H' Class 0–4–4T No 31544 heads away from Tunbridge Wells west on a summer afternoon with the 3 pm auto train for Oxted. Immediately behind the train is the engine shed with Standard 2–6–4T No 80011 standing alongside. 3 June 1961.

and the aforementioned joint LB&SCR/SER Croydon to Oxted line of 1884 used some of the earthworks of the Surrey & Sussex Junction.

In the late 1870s, an SER scheme to link Tunbridge Wells with Hailsham and thus gain access to Eastbourne provoked the Brighton company into taking over and building a line from Eridge, on its Tunbridge Wells to Lewes route, to Hailsham. It opened in September 1880, and the SER was granted running powers; for a very short time the company tried out a Charing Cross to Eastbourne service, but hardly anybody bothered to use it so the LB&SCR could sleep easily again.

Four last pieces of this many-linked chain remain to be recorded. All would provide further routes between London and Brighton although the amount of use made of them for this purpose would vary greatly. In September 1883, a 4½-miles-long line was built linking the East Grinstead to Lewes line at Horsted Keynes with the main London to Brighton line at Haywards Heath. Horsted Keynes was quite an impressive junction station with four through lines and three platforms, but was a fair old march from the village after which it was named.

In August 1885, the Woodside & South Croydon Railway opened. This was a joint LB&SCR/SER affair, but was very much to the advantage of the latter for it provided an alternative route from London to the Kent coast by way of Oxted and the Crowhurst curve and also brought the tantalizing prospect of access to Brighton a little nearer. Something less than three years later, in October 1888, a line from Hurst Green Junction, south of Oxted, was opened through Edenbridge to Ashurst Junction on the East Grinstead to Tunbridge Wells line.

The very last link takes us into the twentieth century when the long-delayed but important Ashurst Spur between the Oxted and East Grinstead to Tunbrige Wells and the Tunbridge Wells to Eastbourne and Brighton lines between Ashurst Junction and Birchden Junction on the Kent/Sussex border was completed in June 1914. The significance of this was that there was now a shorter route between Croydon and Eastbourne than the main line via Keymer Junction and it was also yet another practicable alternative Croydon to Brighton route. In fact, although the original London to Brighton and Eastbourne main lines were never challenged, through trains between London and the two resorts continued to run down the Oxted line and over the Ashurst Spur into the 1960s, maintaining, for those who relished such curiosities, regular steam-hauled travel between London and the principal Sussex resorts for some 30 years after the main lines had been electrified.

BRIGHTON CONTRASTS

The original Brighton station soon proved too small for the ever increasing traffic it was called upon to handle. Clearly it had to be enlarged, but as at the other end of the line at Victoria, there was no room to extend on either side and therefore there could be no extra platforms. The only solution was to lengthen them. It was not ideal but it did mean that two trains could be accommodated at the same platform. Special signalling arrangements had to be made, a task naturally enough put in the capable hands of Saxby and Farmer. Because the platforms were now so long, only the most westerly ones could give access to the westward coast line.

The engineer responsible in a consultant capacity for designing the rebuilt station was H. E. Wallis, who had also worked for the LC&DR. The Chief Resident Engineer of the LB&SCR who oversaw the works was Jacomb-Wood's successor, Fred Bannister. It was a position he held for the remarkably long time of 36 years, from 1860 to 1896. Bannister had started on the railway in 1846, under Jacomb-Wood, but had then gone into

Brighton station in 1905. An 'E5' 0–6–2T awaits the right away (Brighton Libraries).

A Robert Billinton-designed 'C2' Class 0–6–0 finds itself promoted to passenger work and approaches Preston Park with a Victoria to Brighton excursion made up of Stroudley four-wheelers, circa 1900 (Stent Collection, Brighton Libraries).

private practice in Brighton where he was involved in many schemes during the period of the town's greatest expansion, being concerned with the 'building of model dwellings for the labouring classes'.

At one point during the station rebuilding work, the Board of Directors got it into their collective head that Bannister wasn't keeping a close enough eye upon Wallis and had the latter dismissed. As an article in the *Railway Magazine* in March 1988 by Michael Bannister, a descendant of Fred Bannister, recalled, there were calls for Bannister's head too. However, he survived and in fact re-employed Wallis in the years 1878–82. By 1883, the work was finished and although it had cost more than double Bannister's original estimate — £50,000 as against £24,000 — which probably explains the Board's sudden fit of nervousness, Wallis and Bannister and the men under them had done a splendid job.

The magnificent curving roof gave Brighton the finest station of any resort in the kingdom. There were those who considered that the extensive iron and glass awning added to Mocatta's handsome facade spoiled the external view, but that is not the author's opinion and the convenience of a spacious, covered, direct approach from Queen Street was vastly to the benefit of travellers.

As the nineteenth century drew to a close the character of Brighton was changing, and in the 'Naughty Nineties' was quite different from that of the select spa town favoured by royalty and the smart set 60 years earlier. It was 'London by the sea', and it reproduced all the vices and virtues of the capital, the 'greatest city in the world'. Whilst the affluent middle and upper classes travelled down in the greatest comfort in Pullman cars and stayed in the Metropole or the Grand, the lower orders would bounce down in a Stroudley four-wheeler and stay in a boarding house such as Hilda Lessways had charge of in Preston Street when Edwin Clayhanger rediscovered her.

'It was shabby. All its tints had merged by use and by time into one tint, nondescript and unpleasant, in which yellow prospered. The fireplace was draped; the door was draped; the back of the piano was draped; and some of the dark suspicious stuffs showed a clear pattern. The faded chairs were hidden by faded antimacassars; the little futile tables concealed their rickets under vague needlework, on which were displayed in straw or tinsel frames pale portraits of dowdy people who had stood like sheep before fifteenth-rate photographers.'

Edwin himself, a successful owner of a printing works in the Five Towns, is staying at the Royal Sussex Hotel, a vastly superior

'Gladstone' Class 0–4–2 No 198 Sheffield *on the main line with a train of umber and white liveried bogie carriages,* circa 1910. *No 198 was amongst the longest lived of her class, being built in December 1887 and withdrawn 44 years later by the Southern Railway in 1931* (Lens of Sutton).

establishment. He gets into conversation with 'an old Jew . . . drinking tea at a Moorish table'. The lounge in which they are sitting is crowded.

'Hope had sent down from London trains full of people whose determination was to live and to see life in a grandiose manner. All about the lounge of the Royal Sussex were groups of elegant youngish men and flaxen, uneasily stylish women, inviting the assistance of flattered waiters to decide what liqueurs they should have next.'

The Royal Pavilion mirrored the varying fortunes of the town. Liberty's spent no less than £2,000 on soft decorations for a Maharajah's Ball held there, but these could not prevent the Prince of Wales commenting, in 1896, on 'the Pavilion's faded appearance'. The late Victorian and Edwardian era was not one of impeccable good taste, and in many directions florid opulence was preferred to elegance and restraint. The London, Brighton & South Coast Railway, however, generally managed to steer clear of the worst excesses of the period and its locomotives, carriages and buildings were well designed and stood the test of time. Stroudley's nineteenth-century yellow livery for locomotives gave way to an attractive and dignified umber, main line carriages had their upper panels painted white, and the new suburban stations built when extra tracks were provided on the main line between East Croydon and Victoria were, and to quite an extent remain, solidly handsome.

STROUDLEY AND BILLINTON

The old engineering adage that if it looks right it is right is sadly not always true, but for all that there have been many excellent engineers who knew how to produce a handsome machine. Amongst the most distinguished was William Stroudley. Every design of his was a work of art, and although by the late 1890s the increasing weight and size of bogie carriages seemed to render his locomotives out of date and undersized, many continued to find useful employment not just into Southern Railway days but into the British Railways era too. Today, no fewer than 12 still exist, each one over 100 years old. For a locomotive designer who was dead by 1889, this is a unique distinction.

It hardly needs to be said that the colour of a locomotive is a superficial finishing touch which can have no bearing on its performance and efficiency. Yet because Stroudley's engines wore what was surely the most distinctive livery ever to be applied within these islands, one is just a little surprised to discover that their mechanical virtues were such that they would probably be almost as well remembered if they had been painted a dull grey instead of the remarkable yellow ochre which Stroudley chose to call 'improved engine green'.

A native of Oxfordshire, who had worked at Swindon, Peterborough and Cowlairs, Stroudley imported the colour from the Highland Railway, where he had been the Locomotive and Carriage Superintendent, and it attracted vastly more attention when applied to engines running between the capital and the Sussex coast than it ever did around the shores of the Moray Firth. Each driver was allocated his own engine; the roofs were painted white, and for a number of services, the best remembered being the Newhaven boat train, the driver was treated virtually as an independent agent. He was given an agreed sum, out of which he paid the fireman and the cleaners, the rest being his wages. Such responsibility and independence ensured that a driver often regarded his engine as virtually his own property and kept it in immaculate condition. It was a system which worked well in Victorian times, when the status of a main line engine driver was equivalent to that of a modern airline pilot, when wages were a relatively small proportion of running costs, and when a locomotive was expected to cover what would in modern terms be considered a ludicrously small daily mileage.

Stroudley's engines were immediately recognized as being greatly in advance of anything Craven had ever produced for the Brighton line. One of Stroudley's first actions on taking over at Brighton was to have Fred Bannister, the Chief Engineer, prepare a plan for rebuilding the works and this was put into effect over a period of years. (It is worth noting that the immaculate condition of Stroudley's yellow engines did not prevent Brighton Corporation complaining about the severe pollution caused by the smoking chimneys of the works.)

The much improved machinery with which Stroudley and Bannister equipped the works enabled the former to design engines where every detail was carefully considered in the knowledge that each part would be made to the highest specifications. The result was that Stroudley locomotives in their heyday did all that was asked of them economically and efficiently; long after, when they had been superseded by much larger machines, they were still able to perform astonishing feats of haulage, while in later years their light weight and sound construction also made them ideal for branch line work where bigger engines would have been inefficient and unnecessary.

The most famous were the 0–6–0T 'Terriers', officially 'A1' Class. Their nickname was most appropriate, for they were

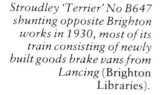

Stroudley 'Terrier' No B647 shunting opposite Brighton works in 1930, most of its train consisting of newly built goods brake vans from Lancing (Brighton Libraries).

small, tough and appealing. They are so familiar — ten have been preserved — and so much has been written about them that it is hardly necessary to go into much detail here. There were 50 in all, built at Brighton between 1872 and 1881. They weighed 24 tons 14 cwt in working order, and the great majority originally worked on suburban services in the London area, although there were always some of the class at Brighton shed.

The Brighton made a greater use of tank engines than any other main line company in the country. The chief reason was that a tank engine could accomplish the 50 miles between London and Brighton quite comfortably, without taking on more coal and water, so why build a more expensive tender engine which had to be turned out at the end of each run? Thus no fewer than 125 'D1' 0–4–2Ts were turned out between 1874 and 1887 and they became maids of all work on the Brighton system. A number went to Brighton shed and worked stopping and semi-fast trains to London and elsewhere.

Stroudley's third tank engine design was the 'E1' Class 0–6–0T. Considerably larger than the 'Terriers', an 'E1' in working order weighed 39 tons 10 cwt. It was principally a goods engine, and was therefore painted dark green, and the first, No 97, emerged in November 1874 and was put to work at Brighton shed where she was joined by many of her sisters.

Despite this mass production of tank engines, the Brighton still regarded tender engines as the only suitable motive power for the

The Stroudley-designed 'A1' Class 'Terrier' 0–6–0T No 58 Wandle *built in October 1875 and broken up in February 1902.*

A 'G' Class single of 1880 entering East Croydon with a down train, circa 1900 (Brighton Libraries).

heaviest goods and the most important passenger trains. Stroudley designed two types of 0–6–0, and both, at the time of their introduction, were the most powerful goods engines in the country. The 20 'Cs' came out between 1871 and 1874, and their successors, the 'C1s', of which there were 12, appeared between 1882 and 1887.

Stroudley's first venture in the express engine field was a splendid 'single', No 151, later No 326 *Grosvenor*, which appeared in 1874. She was fitted with a particularly large boiler for her time and for some while had charge of the crack 5.00 pm London Bridge to Brighton businessmen's express. Other, smaller, 2–2–2s followed, the 'F' and 'G' Classes; the 'Gs' were the last 'singles' to run on the LB&SCR, and the last survivor, No 329 *Stephenson*, was withdrawn in 1914.

Stroudley did not like bogies, and when he decided to bring out a coupled passenger tender engine he chose the 0–4–2 wheel arrangement. First of these was a tender version of the 'D1' tank, the 'D2', of which 20 were built. Next came the six larger-wheeled 'D3s'. They were perfectly good, worthy machines, although they did not last particularly long, being scrapped after some 20 years and being outlived by many of the 'singles'.

But these were merely the precursors of the best-remembered of all Stroudley's tender engines, the 'B1s', or, as they were much better known, the 'Gladstones'. No 214 *Gladstone* himself came out of Brighton works just in time for Christmas 1882; there was no hurry to get him into service, so he did not take up work until the new year. After extensive trials, the Board of Directors and Stroudley pronounced themselves well satisfied and another 35 of the class were completed between December 1883 and April 1891.

The 'Gladstones, were superb-looking engines. They had large boilers for their time, although not so big that there wasn't room for an impressive copper-capped chimney and dome surmounted by Salter safety valves, boldly curving splashers over the 6 ft 6 in driving wheels, and a most elegant sweep down from the cab to the running plate. The Stroudley tender with its inside bearings and lack of coal rails was particularly simple and elegant, and whilst it looked well behind any engine, it might have been designed especially for the 'Gladstones'.

The 'Gladstones' were as good as they looked, and for decades performed splendid work on the Brighton main line. The last, No 172 *Littlehampton*, which was built in April 1891, over a year after her creator's death, was the last to be taken out of service, in 1933. But she was not the last survivor, and the story of the preservation of *Gladstone* himself, an event which was to have a significance far beyond the important and most happy rescue of a fine engine, will be told in a later chapter.

So proud was the LB&SCR of its beautiful yellow ochre engines that it sent various of them to attend international exhibitions where they invariably won medals. The company had particular links with France through its cross-Channel services, and

Gladstone as restored at Brighton Works, seen at Nine Elms in May 1927 before going for display at York Museum (LPC).

it was whilst on a visit to Paris with the 'Gladstone' Class engine *Edward Blount* in December 1889 that Stroudley suddenly became ill. Within three days, to everyone's consternation and sorrow, he was dead. A tremendous funeral was held for him, the procession through the streets of Brighton to the Extra-mural Cemetery being over half a mile long and including some 1,600 employees of Brighton works. He was 56, and the editor of *The Engineer* wrote that his 'untimely death leaves a blank in the ranks of engineers that will never really be filled'.

But of course there had to be a successor. That man was Robert John Billinton. A 45-year-old Yorkshireman, he had worked with Stroudley at Brighton as his assistant from 1870 to 1874, and after that had spent 16 years as Chief Draughtsman at the vast Derby Works of the Midland Railway. Consequently, when he came back to Brighton in 1890 he not only understood Brighton ways but was a highly experienced engineer and designer.

The Midland Railway was fond of 0–4–4Ts and it was not surprising that Billinton's first design was of this wheel arrangement, particularly as the LB&SCR's southern neighbours also favoured the type. Classified 'D3', the first, No 363 *Goldsmid* (later *Havant*), came out of Brighton works in May 1892, to be followed by 34 others. Painted in Stroudley's yellow livery and perpetuating his cab and tanks, the 'D3s', despite their connections with the far-away Midland, were happily accepted into the Brighton ranks and proved to be useful and long-lived engines. They were familiar on virtually every type of passenger service;

Hamilton Ellis recalls travelling to school behind one which regularly worked the 4.5 pm from Victoria via Horsham and the Steyning branch to Shoreham to Brighton.

Although Stroudley had established the tradition of the LB&SCR as a tank engine line, a tradition which would continue for the rest of the company's existence, the wheel arrangement which in some ways epitomized the LB&SCR emerged in later days — this was 0–6–2T. Billinton's various engines of this type never aspired to the limelight, or if they did no one noticed and it was not achieved. Yet they were immensely useful and served the company and its two successors long and faithfully.

First, in 1894–5, came the 'E3s' which were modifications of the lone Stroudley 0–6–2T *West Brighton*. There were 16 of them, 17 with the Stroudley engine, and although intended for goods traffic they proved so useful on suburban passenger work that no fewer than 74 of a similar design, but with larger 5 ft coupled driving wheels, were produced purely for passenger work. These were the 'E4s', built between 1897 and 1903, and for some reason the majority, but not all, were painted yellow.

The 0–6–2T wheel arrangement may not seem ideal for fast passenger work but so enamoured of it was Billinton that in 1902 he brought out his 5 ft 6 in 'E5s'. The class numbered 30 and proved perfectly capable of handling, if not the most prestigious main line expresses, then many sharply timed quite long-distance passenger services.

Last of all was the 'E6'. Possibly the most unassuming of the lot, the 12 engines of the class spent their days on short-distance and shunting work. So retiring were they that whilst the majority were painted in the usual goods green, the last two appeared in

Two Robert Billinton engines at Norwood Junction in October 1954, No 32543, a 'C2X' 0–6–0 rebuilt by Marsh, and No 32413, an 'E6' 0–6–2T. Although both were at this time stored out of use, they have several more years' work ahead of them.

A 'D3' Class 0–4–4T approaching East Grinstead High Level station with a train from Three Bridges made up of a former SECR birdcage set, circa 1935. The signal is an LB & SCR-built lower quadrant, the last of which survived on the East Grinstead line at Hurst Green until the early 1970s (Author's collection).

black livery whilst the final four were without names. They emerged in 1905, and it was the death of their designer, at Brighton the previous November, which determined their unglamorous appearance.

Billinton was also responsible for a number of tender engine designs. In 1893, Brighton works being fully occupied with the building of tank engines, the Vulcan Foundry at Newton-le-Willows was given the contract of constructing 55 'C2' 0–6–0s. They were clearly related to their Stroudley predecessors and were destined to last in considerable numbers, albeit rebuilt, late into the steam era on the Central section of the Southern Region of British Railways.

Inevitably perhaps, for goods engines tend to have longer lives than express passenger ones, Billinton's 'B2' Class 4–4–0s, which were contemporary with the 'C2s', disappeared well before

British Railways days. A 4–4–0 was something quite new to the
Brighton, but elsewhere — the Midland Railway, for example —
it was the most popular wheel arrangement for express passenger
work, so no one was greatly surprised when the first 'B2', No 314
Charles C. Macrae, was wheeled out of Brighton works in the
summer of 1895. Painted in 'improved engine green', it was an
elegant machine. Mechanically, however, it was nothing very
wonderful. Looking at pictures of the original 'B2s' one is struck
by the smallness of the boiler, and, curiously, the 4–4–0s did not
ride as smoothly as their predecessors, the 'Gladstones', despite
the latter's leading driving wheels, and they came to be known to
the crews which worked them as 'Grasshoppers', which says it

*Marsh 'C3' Class 0–6–0 No
2304 and Robert Billinton
'B4' Class 4–4–0 No 2047
at New Cross depot in 1939
(Author's collection).*

*A 'B4' Class 4–4–0 No 52
Sussex (originally Siemens)
about to depart from
Victoria with a Brighton
express in May 1919.
No 52 was rebuilt in the
early months of the
Southern Railway as a
'B4X', emerging from
Brighton Works in her new
guise in May 1923, and was
withdrawn by British
Railways in December 1951
(Author's collection).*

all. The 24 'B2s' came out between June 1895 and January 1898, then in the same month as the final one, No 212 *Armstrong*, was completed, a larger-boilered but otherwise similar engine, No 213 *Bessemer*, was built, and classified 'B3'. *Bessemer* was clearly no great improvement on the 'B2s' and was destined to remain without brothers or sisters; the real successor to the 'B2' was the 'B4'.

The first 'B4', No 52 *Siemens* (later *Sussex*), emerged from Brighton works around Christmas 1899, just in time to welcome the new century. She was to have 32 sisters, the majority of them built by Sharp, Stewart and Co of Glasgow, hence the nickname 'Scotchmen', one which would also be applied to a later generation of Southern express engines, the 'King Arthurs' built by the North British Company.

LB&SCR tank engines were usually named after places served by the company, but tender engines were not, although anyone studying the names of the 'B4s' might have thought they were; No 71, for example, was named *Goodwood*, whilst No 72 was *Sussex* and No 73 *Westminster*. (There were some companies, the GWR for instance, which thought nothing of hijacking names from other people's territories, but surely the LB&SCR naming 'B4' No 63 *Mafeking* was going a bit far?) In fact, the names bestowed upon the 'B4s' give the impression of being the result of the efforts of a very early, possibly steam-operated, computer which developed a malfunction, or rather several, long before it reached number 33! The Boer War and jingoism being at their height, one can understand why many of the locomotives had names associated with this conflict, but there was also an engineer (left over from the 'B2' series one supposes), various bits of the Empire, royal residences in various parts of the country, various bits of the royal family itself, and *Bagshot*. (*Bagshot*? Possibly a preliminary skirmish with the Boers took place there . . .) In any event the medley of names survived until Marsh came along with his brown paintbrush and wiped them out, along with practically all other Brighton names, in the first decade of the twentieth century, although *Bagshot* lasted, nameless, until 1934.

Billinton's death, although occurring four years into the new century, brought about the end of the Victorian era as far as Brighton locomotive affairs were concerned. Not only was yellow now decreed an unsuitable livery, but the engines which came out in Marsh's dignified but vastly less opulent umber brown had a massive, although still handsome, appearance which would have been inconceivable in Victorian times.

LUXURY UNLIMITED

Brighton fell out of favour with Queen Victoria early on in her reign. She had the Prince Regent's Royal Pavilion systematically stripped of its magnificent appointments until it was nothing but a shell, and in March 1849 a Bill was put before Parliament to enable it to be demolished and the site sold; the money realized from this prime piece of land in the heart of the resort would go towards repairs and improvements at Buckingham Palace. Whilst the citizens of Brighton (most of them) sympathized with the Queen's desire to prevent rain seeping through the royal slates into the royal porridge, they made it clear that they considered there must be means of raising a mortgage other than the demolition of their most famous building, so the town offered the crown £53,000 for the Pavilion. It was accepted, and after much restoration work a grand ball was held in January 1851, the year of the Great Exhibition, to celebrate the new era.

'B4' 4–4–0 No 42 His Majesty *returning from Portsmouth Harbour with the Royal Train with Edward VII on board* (Brighton Library).

Royalty returned in 1866 when the Prince of Wales paid a visit, and he and many other members of the British and other royal families attended various balls and state occasions there over the years. So although Queen Victoria herself neither visited Brighton nor travelled over LB&SCR tracks in the latter decades of the nineteenth century, the company felt itself justified in building a complete Royal Train in 1897, principally for the use of the Prince of Wales. Its five carriages were vastly superior to anything the company had, or would ever build for its ordinary customers. However, it had one archaic feature in common with contemporary main-line stock, and that was a lack of gangway connections, but this was done on the express wish of the Prince. Otherwise it was splendidly up-to-date with clerestory roofs, electric lighting, engraved glass, lavatories and leather-upholstered seating, and was finished externally in varnished mahogany.

In fact, Queen Victoria did travel in it — once. She died at Osborne on the Isle of Wight, the house designed by her beloved Albert, at the end of January 1901, and her body, instead of being brought to London by the LSWR route which she had favoured in life, was brought to Gosport, conveyed by the LSWR as far as Fareham, and there handed over to the LB&SCR. 'B4' No 54 *Empress* was in charge and three extra carriages were provided, one of these being the GWR funeral car. What followed was a remarkable journey. For various reasons, the train left 9 minutes late, and the LB&SCR's Outdoor Locomotive Superintendent reminded the driver, Walter Cooper, that the new King was a stickler for punctuality. No further urging was needed. The old Queen had always insisted that no train she travelled in should ever exceed 40 mph, but her mortal remains now found themselves travelling at more than twice that speed. The 9 minutes late departure was turned into a 2 minutes early arrival at Victoria, and to achieve this there must have been places where speed restrictions were exceeded quite liberally, and this with eight carriage-loads of European royalty, to say nothing of the body of the Queen Empress. Kaiser Wilhelm of Germany, Queen Victoria's nephew and one of the passengers, was thrilled, and sent a minion to congratulate the crew.

One of the subsequent regular duties of the Royal Train was to convey Edward VII to Epsom for the Derby; it was also much used for journeys in connection with naval events at Portsmouth.

By the end of the nineteenth century, bogie carriages were being turned out in some numbers by the LB&SCR, both for express and suburban work, and in 1903 a change of livery saw the appearance of main-line carriages with white upper panels

which made them a nice match for the Pullmans. By this time the LB&SCR was recognized as the leading light in Pullman travel. Not only were complete Pullman trains being run, but individual cars were being provided on an increasing scale as restaurant and lounge cars on many of the expresses between Victoria and London Bridge and the coast. It is easy to criticise the Brighton for building carriages of a somewhat archaic design, but this must be always balanced against the fact that Pullman cars were an everyday feature of the principal expresses, providing an unequalled standard of comfort.

The umber and cream livery, which as far as most people are concerned is *the* Pullman livery, did not actually appear until 1906 when three cars, 'Duchess of Norfolk', 'Princess Ena' and 'Princess Patricia' emerged from Brighton works so attired. In fact, this colour scheme was applied to LB&SCR carriages first, and the new Pullmans were painted to match it, not the other way round.

And so we come to the most famous Brighton line express. On 1 November 1908, the 'Southern Belle' 'made its bow to the public as the first daily all-Pullman train in the country!', to quote the *Railway Magazine* of December 1929, marking the train's 21st anniversary. It went on to note that 'The credit for the

The 'Pullman No 1 Train' consisting of three cars, 'Prince', 'Princess' and 'Albert Victor', built at Pullman City, Illinois, re-assembled at Brighton works and put into service in 1888. The leading vehicle is a six-wheel van housing all the generating equip-ment, as well as the guard and the passengers' luggage. Although not a real Pullman, it was designed to match the three bogie cars and soon became known as a 'Pullman Pup'. The re-mainder of the train is made up of ordinary carriages. The locomotive is a 'Gladstone', and the picture was taken around the turn of the century near Purley (Author's collection).

inauguration of so revolutionary a service belonged primarily to the late Lord Dalziel (then Mr Davison Dalziel), a pioneer of de luxe railway travel, and secondly to the Board of the London, Brighton and South Coast Railway for their enterprise in so readily supporting him'.

Dalziel had bought the British Pullman company in 1907 and having persuaded the LB&SCR to introduce the 'Southern Belle' he had had the very first all-British Pullman cars built at the Lancaster works of the Metropolitan Amalgamated Carriage and Wagon Company. These seven cars, with their high elliptical roofs and umber and cream livery, set the style for all subsequent Pullmans down to the 1950s. They had six-wheel bogies and were heavier than any of their predecessors, and naturally the interiors were splendid.

To quote the *Railway Magazine* again: 'The new train was an instantaneous success. Nothing like it had been offered to the everyday travelling public before; the luxury of the cars, the beauty of the decorations, the ease of riding, the fine quality of the cuisine, the courtesy of the staff, and, finally, the splendid speed of the train, combined to lift it right out of the ordinary, and place it among those favoured few which have gained world fame.' For the first two years of its existence, the 'Southern Belle' did one journey down in the morning and returned to London in the evening, but its popularity was such that in 1910 this schedule was doubled.

TOWARDS A NEW CENTURY

ondon Bridge station had needed enlarging and improving
almost as soon as it was built, and it rapidly grew into the
extensive and somewhat rambling establishment familiar to
generations of business gents until the Luftwaffe knocked it
about, leaving it even more rambling, and until British Rail took
it in hand in the late 1970s and 80s. The company's West End
terminus, Victoria, being much newer, was constructed on rather
more generous lines, but the time came when it too could no
longer cope with the traffic trying to get in and out of it.

It was around this time, incidentally, that Victoria made its
most famous fictional appearance, for in 1895 Oscar Wilde's *The
Importance of Being Earnest* was published. In it Wilde has one
of the heroes, Jack Worthing, discovered as a baby in a bag in the
left luggage office. When Jack explains that it was the Brighton
line office, which is how he acquired his surname, the formidable
Lady Bracknell makes her famous remark that 'the line is
immaterial'. Which is not a view a passenger bound for Bognor
who found himself on a Ramsgate train would share.

Some 11 years before Oscar Wilde made the left luggage office
famous, a very different event propelled it into the headlines. An
explosion at three minutes past one on the morning of 25
February 1884 destroyed it, along with the first class waiting
room and inspector's office next door, and other areas of the
station were also damaged. Fortunately there were only five men
on duty, the last train having already arrived, and of these two
porters were hurt, one seriously. Mr Manning, the Night
Inspector, managed to put out the subsequent fire just as the
brigade was arriving. The package containing the bomb which
caused the explosion had been brought in at around 8.30 pm
the previous evening. Ticking was heard coming from it, but the
depositors explained that it was a parcel of clocks and instructed
the porters not to put anything on top of it. The *Illustrated
London News* reported that it was generally believed that the
perpetrators were 'Fenian conspirators' and that their intention
was to 'frighten the people of London'. At this time, Gladstone

The building of the Inner Circle line by the cut-and-cover method (Author's collection).

was attempting to get Parliament to grant Ireland home rule, but despite his most valiant efforts he failed. Had he succeeded, the Victoria incident of 1884 would have been an isolated one instead of becoming one of the first pieces of a deadly pattern which has become so familiar in the succeeding 100 years on both sides of the Irish Sea.

A significant contributor to Victoria station's ever-increasing business was the Underground. The first underground railway in London, the Metropolitan, had opened between Bishop's Head, Paddington, and Farringdon Street in 1863, and such was its success that within a year no fewer than 259 schemes were being proposed for similar railways within the Metropolis; granted this was rather excessive, but a number nevertheless went ahead. One of their prime objects was to link up the main-line stations to not only provide a much quicker and more efficient method of travelling between them than struggling in horse-drawn vehicles through the overcrowded streets, but to also compete successfully with the various often circuitous surface links which the main-line companies had provided between their systems.

The Inner Circle line was proposed by the Metropolitan District Railways in 1863. It received parliamentary approval, work began, and on Christmas Eve 1868 the first section, from South Kensington by way of Victoria to Westminster Bridge, opened for business. Its construction caused as great an upheaval in the districts through which it passed as an ordinary surface line would have done, for it was built on the 'cut-and-cover' principle which meant that the street below which it was going to run was dug up, the line was constructed, the rails laid, and the whole thing covered up again. This happened in Victoria Street, for instance, and the dislocation to traffic which wanted to pass up and down it, to say nothing of the noise, was fearful. All later schemes were deep-level 'tubes', and by comparison their arrival was hardly noticed. However, it would be more than 100 years before the tube reached Victoria.

At this point Brunel re-enters our story. Father and son, Marc and Isambard, had, with immense difficulty and on one occasion with almost fatal results for Isambard, built the first tunnel under the Thames between Rotherhithe and Wapping. Although one of the wonders of the age, it had not been a financial success and since its completion in 1843 had been used only by foot passengers. Some 20 years later, a railway was promoted to pass through the Thames Tunnel and in the fullness of time it was constructed and began running in December 1869 from a station alongside that of the LB&SCR at New Cross (now New Cross Gate) to Wapping. The history of the East London line, as it became known, and its various connections is fascinating and complicated, but we do not have space to go into it save to note that originally the LB&SCR agreed to receive 53% of the gross receipts and that shortly the line was extended northwards to connect with both the Great Eastern Railway and the rest of the Underground system, and southwards to the South Eastern Railway at New Cross.

One of the original District Line wooden-bodied Underground motor cars, dating from 1910 and once used on the Inner Circle, at New Cross Gate on 28 August 1947 being passed by a former SECR 'L' Class 4–4–0 on the 1.09 pm London Bridge to Brighton van train (Madgwick Collection, Brighton Libraries).

New Cross Gate in 1969. The Underground train about to depart over the East London line to Whitechapel has clerestory-roofed motor cars, the very last such vehicles to remain in ordinary service in the British Isles. Beyond the British Rail sidings are the commercial and residential buildings of the nineteenth and twentieth century docklands.

All sorts of services, worked by a number of companies, have used the line over the years, but since its electrification in March 1913 it has generally been regarded as part of the Underground system, although the physical connection with British Rail remained at New Cross Gate until the 1960s. Today, East London line trains, although run as a self-contained section of the Underground, use the Network SouthEast stations at New Cross Gate and New Cross and provide a useful connection for passengers to the rapidly developing Docklands area and East London generally.

Gradually the Inner Circle was extended. It had been intended that there would be a link at West Brompton (Lillie Bridge) with the West London Extension Railway so that LB&SCR and LSWR trains could run over the Underground lines, but this never happened. In May 1870, the eastwards extension past Charing Cross to Blackfriars came into use, and that to Cannon Street and Mansion House just over a year later. Other lines were being built, and by the time the final section completing the Inner Circle was opened in July 1884, Victoria was linked by underground not only to all the main-line stations but to many other parts of London and its suburbs too.

Of course London's underground railways were all originally steam operated. I have a delightful Thomas Nelson children's book, given to my father when he was a small boy at the turn of the century, and in it a family are setting off for their seaside holiday from their home at Richmond. Doris asks 'what the words "Inner Circle" meant, which she saw painted upon a board in front of an engine that had gone past'. Grandpapa explains and then Amy complains, 'But why do they have these horrid underground railways at all? The smoke hurts my eyes, and I am nearly choked, and I cannot see anything out of the window.'

Electrification was to be the answer to Amy's, and lots of others' complaints, and the man who brought it about was an American. Charles Tyson Yerkes came from Chicago, and having bought up and electrified the tramways of his own city, he decided to extend his empire to the other side of the Atlantic. Amongst his acquisitions was the Metropolitan District Railway. He immediately went ahead with electrifying all its routes, a process which was completed by 1905. This, as we shall see, was to have no small influence on the London, Brighton & South Coast Railway, but let us, for the moment, return to the rebuilding of Victoria station.

By the end of the nineteenth century, land values and the density of occupation in the West End of London were such that the widening of Victoria station, either across Buckingham

A 'D' stock District Line train, dating from 1980, at Victoria on a Richmond service.

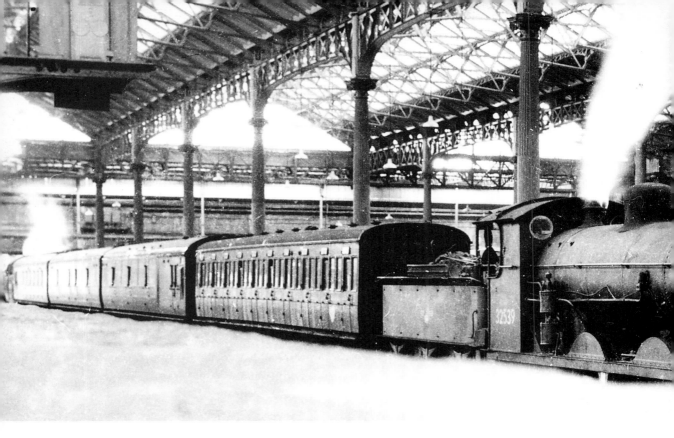

Former LB & SCR 'C2X' Class 0-6-0 No 32539 with the empty stock of an Oxted line train at the extension to platform 15 at Victoria, in August 1961. The area inhabited by the parcels porters (which that summer included the author) is seen on the opposite side of the platform with the leading Pullman of the 'Brighton Belle' just visible between the road vans and the pile of parcels.

Palace Road or out over the forecourt, was quite out of the question. This left as the only option the lengthening of the platforms so that, with the appropriate pointwork and signalling, each could accommodate two trains at the same time. The next-door-neighbours, the South Eastern Railway, were consulted at an early stage and on 10 November 1898 wrote to the LB&SCR that 'more and shorter platforms would be most convenient'. This was generally agreed to, which is rather curious considering that the result was vastly longer platforms.

At the end of that year, the South Eastern and the London, Chatham & Dover companies came together to form the South Eastern & Chatham Joint Committee, whilst at the same time William Forbes, Traffic Manager of the LC&DR, moved to the LB&SCR to become its General Manager. He was to hold this position for the rest of the company's existence and as such is one of the most important figures in the history of the LB&SCR. He it was who oversaw the rebuilding of Victoria and inaugurated electrification.

The extension of Victoria inevitably caused much upheaval to the neighbours, most of whom gracefully accepted financial compensation. The minute book of the Board of Directors of the LB&SCR records that on 27 July 1898 the General Manager was authorized to negotiate with the Duke of Westminster over the purchase of land. The result was that most of the Grosvenor

A once common sight when almost all of London's milk arrived by train. A milk churn and LB & SCR van at Sheffield Park.

Canal basin was bought, reducing the canal itself to not much more than a dock. The Vestry of St George's, Hanover Square, received £3,000 for some strips of pavement and 'possible damage to the Public Library and St George's Baths fronting Buckingham Palace Road', various other owners and occupiers of property in Buckingham Palace Road received a total of £1,000, whilst the National School of Cookery hit the jackpot with £26 5s 0d. Rather larger sums were involved in the purchase of the Grosvenor Hotel which, after a good old haggle, was brought for £230,000. If only its owners could have consulted the LB&SCR minute books they would have seen that the company was prepared to go up to a £$\frac{1}{4}$ million!

In January 1904 a letter was received from the secretary of the Architectural Vigilance Society 'expressing the hope that the design and elevation of the new station buildings would be of artistic merit'. It went on to suggest various alterations to the plans, but the Board replied that it had its own 'competent architect' and that in any case it was too late. This latter statement was a dreadful fib for it was not until June of that year that the Board considered and agreed to the plans for the front elevation of the station. They made one amendment, that the facade, instead of being a mixture of brick and stone, should be made entirely of Portland stone. The engineer's photograph of the casting of the coat of arms which was to be carved on the

Outside porters at Victoria in the 1960s. These were officially retired but there was a gentleman's understanding that they had exclusive rights to continue to carry the luggage of passengers arriving by taxi on the Brighton side. Woe betide any young upstart who unwittingly encroached upon this holy territory.

exterior walls was inspected on 8 February 1905 and approved.

Such concern for the environment, especially the ordinary person's environment, hardly figured in most mid-Victorian's lists of priorities. It was progress, wasn't it, and very little was ever allowed to get in the way of that sacred cow. There were, incidentally, a lot of cows still living in the City of Westminster at that time, often in hardly less hygenic conditions than the lower classes of human inhabitants, but the arrival of the railways meant that all the fresh milk London needed could be brought in from the country. A great impetus to the abolition of the London cow was the outbreak of rinderpest in 1865, and as with foot-and-mouth today, the only way of dealing with this disease was slaughter. Virtually every cow disappeared from London, and the Express Dairy, which had been founded in 1864, expanded its business enormously. Soon almost all of London's milk arrived by train, a situation which continued until the General Strike of 1926.

The nearest open space to Victoria, then as now, was St

James's Park. Today it is perhaps the most attractive of all London's many green areas, a natural oasis screened by tall trees from the government buildings of Whitehall and Downing Street, and St James's and Buckingham palaces, with its lake and its many water birds, and office workers relaxing on the seats and grass. In Victorian times it was very different. Henry James described it thus: 'Its character comes from its nearness to the Westminster slums. There are few hours when a thousand smutty children are not sprawling over it, and the unemployed lie thick on the grass and cover the benches with a brotherhood of greasy corduroys'.

But returning to the new station, a matter which it is felt ought not to be lost to future generations, and is thus recorded here, is that on 15 July 1903 it was agreed that the Metropolitan District Railway would take over the old porters' room used by the LB&SCR, the SECR and the Metropolitan Railways as a storeroom, would provide a new porters' room in the adjoining part of the subway, and would pay £1 p.a. to the joint subway account. Now, not many people know of the joint subway account, but, being an old Victoria porter myself, believe me it is of considerable significance!

On 10 February 1907 the Board learned that the new lines over Grosvenor Bridge were functioning and that the splendid new station was all ready. The rateable value of the property as far as the centre of Grosvenor Bridge was now £34,000, an increase of £247.

In June 1908, George Wright, Superintendent (ordinary stations had to make do with a stationmaster) of Victoria retired due to ill health, and it was agreed that his pension of £278 11s 0d should be made up to £300. He was succeeded by the London Bridge Superintendent, Henry Tickner, who was to receive a salary of £325 p.a. plus a house at 112 Buckingham Palace Road, (fancy being able to boast of such an address!) It is of interest that a move from London Bridge to Victoria was clearly considered a promotion; the West End terminus had established its superiority over the City. Henry Tickner's post was filled by George Jeal, formerly of New Cross Gate, and his salary at London Bridge was to be £215 p.a. plus £40 housing allowance. However, poor Tickner did not last long in the premier position on the line and in November 1910, like his predecessor, ill health forced him to give up; he moved to the rural tranquility of Midhurst. His salary dropped to £115 p.a., but he was allowed to continue to contribute to the pension fund on the basis of the £340 to which his Victoria salary had risen. Jeal succeeded him, but on a salary of only £300.

EARLY ELECTRIFICATION

As the twentieth century opened, steam, which in less than a century had quite transformed the world, was under threat. Petrol and diesel engines, although their potential in railway terms was scarcely realized, had proved their practicality, and a spin in the motor down to Brighton was becoming a favourite outing for young bucks with a mechanical bent. But it was electric traction which was exercising the minds of the boards and the mechanical engineers of many railway compa-

One of the original LCC electric trams, No 106 of 1903, beautifully restored to working order at the National Tramway Museum at Crich in Derbyshire in May 1988. The number '2,412', displayed on the lower panel by the entrance, was the car's official stage carriage number allocated by the licencing authorities.

A Croydon Corporation tram built by Brush in 1906 passing the Swan and Sugar Loaf soon after entering service (Author's collection).

nies. Although Victoria station was one of the first to be served by the Underground, such was the density of the suburban network operated by the main-line companies out of Cannon Street, Charing Cross, London Bridge, Holborn Viaduct, Waterloo and Victoria that the penetration of South London by underground and tube lines was very much less than that north of the Thames. Much more serious competition in the south was offered by the tramways.

The very first horse tram in London ran along Victoria Street. It started work in March 1861 and gave up before the end of the year, but others soon followed. Although rails laid along a busy street could cause all sorts of problems, they also ensured a generally much more comfortable ride than the bus, and many tramway companies sprang up. The largest network was that operated by the London County Council, but it was the London United Tramways which inaugurated electrification, in LSWR territory, in the Shepherds Bush and Brentford areas in April 1901. Before the end of the year, electric trams were running through the streets of Croydon. The LCC quickly followed and its first electrified route took it right through LB&SCR territory, from Westminster to Tooting. Such was the importance of the occasion that the future King George V had charge of the inaugural car. The date was 15 May 1903.

From then on, the vast network of tram routes serving London and its suburbs was electrified with all possible speed. The famous 'E1' type car, which was to last until the very end in 1952,

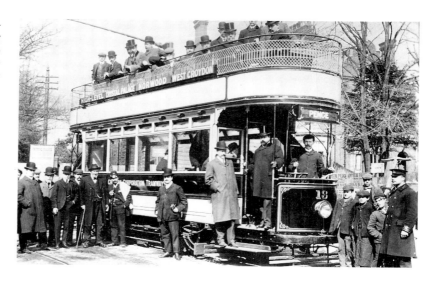

Croydon Corporation four-wheel car No 13 working the West Croydon to Crystal Palace service around the time of the First World War. The posters behind the assorted citizens posing for the camera advertise events at the Crystal Palace (Author's collection).

appeared in 1907. Soon the routes which terminated at Victoria and London Bridge were electrified, and by the end of 1906 the precipitous Anerley Hill had been successfully scaled and Crystal Palace reached.

However, before any of this took place a number of proposals had been put forward for electrified railway lines of one sort or another between London and Brighton, including a monorail whose promoters claimed that a journey time of 20 minutes would be possible. Such claims were by no means far-fetched and the LB&SCR took them seriously. Charles Morgan, the company's Chief Engineer, was sent off to study electrification in Italy and reported back in January 1902 in favour of the overhead system. Despite the threats to its monopoly of the London to Brighton traffic, it was on the suburban lines that the greatest advantage of electrification was expected. As one director, Philip Cardew, previously Electrical Adviser to the Railway Department of the Board of Trade, wrote, the case for electrification centred on a 'much inproved service . . . the trains being more frequent and run on a regular time schedule . . . the mean speed of stopping trains being considerably increased without increase in maximum speed'. Nevertheless, just to show what steam could do on the main line, a special run was organized with 'B4' 4-4-0 No 70 and a lightweight Pullman train on 26 July 1903 which covered the journey from Victoria to Brighton in 48 min 41 sec.

Parliament granted the LB&SCR powers to electrify its lines in the summer of 1903; tenders were invited and, after quite an interval, AEG of Berlin was given the contract to convert the South London line, from Victoria to London Bridge, to the high tension ac single-phase 6,700 volt overhead system.

The work proceeded slowly, but on 17 January 1909 a first, experimental run was made between Battersea Park and East Brixton. Public services were still some way off, but eventually on 1 December 1909 they began, the start of what would become the greatest electrified system in the world. Or was it? The LB&SCR was certainly the first main line company south of the Thames to run electric trains, for the LSWR's did not start until October 1915, and although the SECR took out powers for electrification in 1903, it did not announce its plans until after the First World War was over. But it was the LSWR third rail dc 660 volt system which was eventually chosen by the Southern Railway and perpetuated by the Southern Region of British Railways. So whether the LB&SCR or the LSWR was the true pioneer is open to debate.

An overhead electric from Victoria arriving at Crystal Palace LB & SCR station circa 1920 (Author's collection).

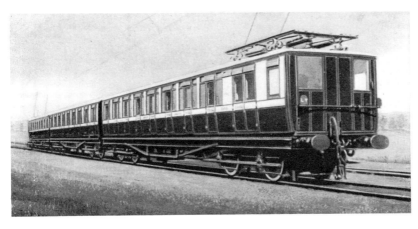

An overhead electric three-car unit poses for its official picture (Author's collection).

Revenue on the South London line, which had slumped alarmingly, recovered rapidly after electrification. From around 8 million passengers in 1903, the numbers had more than halved by 1908; but by 1910 they were back to their 1903 total. The decline cannot be entirely attributed to tramway competition, for the trams' eventual conqueror, the motor bus, began to operate in the streets of London in 1905, whilst a third factor was rising prices and stationary wages which caused a general tightening of belts.

Three-coach trains worked the South London line. Elsewhere in Britain, American-type, and often American-built, open saloon carriages inaugurated electric services, but the Brighton built its own bogie carriages, similar in appearance to its latest steam-hauled stock with a separate door for each compartment. They were, however, provided with side corridors, but no gangway connections between carriages. Built of wood, on massive steel underframes, the roofs and side panels were sheathed in aluminium for safety reasons. The middle, trailer, car was first class; no second class compartments were provided on the trains and from June 1912 all LB&SCR services, other than the Newhaven boat trains, were first and second class only. The amount of first class accommodation provided for the South London trains proved wildly optimistic — goodness knows how the travelling habits of the working class South Londoners could have been so miscalculated. The first class carriages were soon removed, as was their electrical equipment; a lavatory replaced the middle compartment and they found themselves promoted to the fastest Brighton trains, a most curious transformation.

Further electrification soon followed. The ten-miles-long Victoria to Crystal Palace route was next, being inaugurated in May 1911 in time for the Pageant of Empire which was opened by King George V, he who had driven the first LCC electric tram to Tooting. The overhead wires were extended through Norwood Junction to a new depot at Selhurst, situated west of the Selhurst to Norwood Junction loop, and thus electrification reached the county borough of Croydon, although neither East nor West Croydon stations would be reached by the LB&SCR.

In 1913 the company made public its intention to electrify all of its suburban lines as far as Cheam and Coulsdon, but the advent of the First World war immediately cut it off from the suppliers of its electrical equipment. The Peckham Rye to Tulse Hill, Streatham Hill and West Norwood routes had been electrified in June 1912, but it would be the Southern Railway which would complete the work and inaugurate the long-hoped-for electrification of the main line to Brighton.

EDWARDIAN HEYDAY

Robert Billinton, like his predecessor, died in office, on 7 November 1904. His engines may not have achieved the fame of either those of Stroudley or those of Marsh who succeeded him, but for all that we need not doubt that their quality was of the highest order. One simple statistic bears this out; of the 278 locomotives built to Billinton's designs, 80 per cent were still running over 40 years later when the Southern Railway was absorbed by British Railways.

Douglas Earle Marsh had been Chief Assistant Mechanical Engineer of the Great Northern Railway, a company with a tradition of glamorous express engines, and those who hoped that he would remember his inheritance were not disappointed. It has been suggested that Billinton was working on a design for a 4–6–0, but the LB&SCR was destined never to have any engines of that most popular wheel arrangement. Instead, Marsh gave the Brighton something rather more exotic; an 'Atlantic'.

The 'Atlantic' (4–4–2) type was quintessentially Edwardian. Almost all the locomotives of that wheel arrangement which worked on the railways of Britain were built either just before

Marsh 'H1' 'Atlantic' No 39 about to leave London Bridge with a Brighton express shortly after entering service in January 1906 (Author's collection).

that period or during it. They were, without exception, lordly in appearance and were to be seen in charge of such famous expresses as the 'Flying Scotsman', the 'Cornish Riviera' and the 'Southern Belle'. Yet within a decade they were mostly superseded by 'Pacifics' and 4–6–0s, and although many continued to give excellent service for 20 or more years, for the rest of their careers they seemed to epitomize that brief, long-vanished era of supreme self-confidence which evaporated in August 1914.

None of the other Southern lines ever possessed an 'Atlantic', and although the Great Western had some they were soon converted to 4–6–0s, so Marsh's five 'H1s' and six 'H2s' were for most of their careers unique on the lines south of the Thames. The 'H1s' were built in 1905–6 by Kitsons of Leeds, a firm which had supplied the GNR with many of its engines, and their resemblance to Ivatt's Great Northern 'Atlantics' was striking. Their livery was a dark umber; many regretted the passing of Stroudley's yellow ochre, but few could deny how splendid Brighton's new stars looked.

On arrival at Brighton, Marsh had decided that the works needed extensively modernizing, hence the order to Kitsons for the 'Atlantics'. Many thought that they would be too big for any tasks the Brighton could find for them, but they had forgotten the weight of the increasingly popular Pullmans and the generally slow timetabling of all main-line services.

As the nineteenth century drew to an end, the LB&SCR finally grasped the nettle of the Redhill bottleneck and decided to put its altercations with the SECR into history. Quadrupling of much of the main line was put in hand, both in the suburbs and out in the country; the section from Windmill Bridge Junction to Streatham Junction was completed in July 1903, whilst that from South Croydon to Stoat's Nest had come into use in Novemeber 1899. From Stoat's Nest southwards, a completely new line was built, avoiding Redhill. It cut through the grounds of Cane Hill lunatic asylum which necessitated a tunnel, although it was more in the way of a covered cutting, crossed over the Brighton Road, soon to be designated the A23, then passed over the original main line, both being in a deep cutting through the North Downs, before plunging into the 2,113 yards of Quarry Tunnel. Emerging from this into perhaps the most photographed section of the entire Brighton line, it curved gently on a high embankment close to Merstham station on the original line until it reached a third tunnel which took it under the SECR's line at Redhill. From this it continued to Earlswood station where it rejoined the original Brighton line.

The 'Quarry line' was opened in April 1900 and the four-track

SECR 'F1' Class 4–4–0 No 196 climbs the bank near Honor Oak Park with a Reading and Tonbridge train via the old main line to Redhill in 1910. The carriages of the three-coach birdcage set bear destination boards despite being non-corridor vehicles.

section was eventually extended to the mouth of Balcombe Tunnel in 1910. Now at last the Brighton company could make up reasonably fast schedules which it might expect to be kept. 'Reasonably' is the key word, for although one of the new 'Atlantics' reached $86\frac{1}{2}$ mph on a trial run, the company's philosophy was that leaving something in reserve to ensure punctuality was more important than trying to break records. Thus the fastest non-stop service between London Bridge and Brighton in 1882 was 65 minutes, whilst in 1912 the 'Southern Belle' was making each of its four daily runs in exactly one hour. However, these latter were much heavier than any train running 30 years earlier.

The 1912 timetable announced that 'Pullman Drawing Room Cars' were included in no fewer than 17 down trains on Saturdays, two less on Mondays to Fridays, and on six trains on Sundays. Hot meals were served on some of the trains, whilst on the five past midnight out of Victoria, patrons were informed that 'Cold suppers can be served in the Pullman Cars, 2/6 per person' — a supplement of one shilling was charged to each first class passenger occupying a Pullman seat. It was splendid and unique; but then so was Brighton.

The six 'H2' 'Atlantics' emerged from Brighton works in 1911. They were even better looking than the 'H1s', for the running plate was carried in a straight line over the cylinders instead of rising and dipping, but more importantly they were superheated. Marsh was a pioneer of superheating and, as we shall shortly see, his use of it had an influence well beyond the Brighton line. Not only were the 'H2s' fast and powerful but, as a driver of them in their later years once told me, a superheated 'Atlantic' 'would steam with a candle in her firebox'.

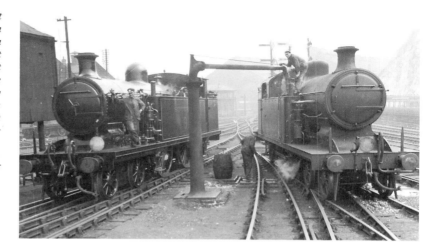

Marsh's output of engines was small, but distinctly interesting;
quality varied from the best forgotten to the outstanding. In the
middle came a small class of 0–6–0s, the 'C3s'. There were only
ten of them, but they lasted some 30 years and are chiefly
remembered for their boiler which, when put on Billinton's 'C2s',
produced the 'C2X' Class which seemed destined to last for ever
and was to be seen all over the old Brighton lines until the 1960s.

Marsh had a great liking for 4–4–2Ts, another imported GNR
wheel arrangement. He built four variations; three of them were
dreadful, but the fourth was one of the finest express engines ever
to run in the British Isles. No amount of research, calculation and
scientific precision can guarantee success to a piece of motive
power, be it a steam engine, a racing car or a spaceship. And to
achieve something out of the ordinary, luck, inspiration and
perhaps the hand of God are also necessary. The 'I1', 'I2' and 'I4'
4–4–2Ts were all very disappointing. They were under-boilered
and suffered from various other faults which various CMEs
attempted to correct over the years, largely without success.

The first of the 'I3' Class, No 21, appeared in 1907, after the
first 'I1s' and 'I2s', although not before the last of them, and
unlike them was intended to be an express rather than a suburban
engine. With its 50–miles-long main line, a tank engine was a
perfectly feasible proposition, as the earlier 0–4–2Ts and
0–6–2Ts had shown. The 'I3' was in many respects a tank engine
version of Billinton's 'B4' 4–4–0, a satisfactory but not outstanding design. No 21 was fast and powerful, but heavy on coal; the
second engine in the class, No 22, was fitted with a Schmidt
superheater, and this was to make a vital difference.

There were 27 'I3s' in all and some were built unsuperheated so that comparisons could be made, although all the class was eventually fitted with the Schmidt apparatus. From the beginning it was clear that the superheated engines were much the most satisfactory, proving to be fast, powerful and economical. That might have been more or less the end of the story with the 'I3s' being noted by the wider world outside the Brighton system as being a handsome engine in the traditions of its line, particularly well suited to the rather special requirements of a railway where tank engines could perform top link express work.

But the 'I3s' achieved fame due to the through workings which brought holidaymakers to Brighton and other south coast destinations from various parts of the London & North Western system by means of what became known as the 'Sunny South Express'. The LB&SCR engine took over from the LNWR at Willesden Junction, and the passage of the express through Surrey and Sussex was watched in awe, for each carriage was gangway-connected to its fellow. The notion of providing a complete train of corridor carriages for ordinary passengers seemed wondrous indeed to the Brighton company's regular clients, while the superior gentleman at Euston must have smirked and felt more confident than ever that his was indeed the Premier Line. Then the LNWR threw all caution to the winds, although assuredly they had no notion they were thus doing, and, having noted that the LB&SCR was providing no more than a reasonably large tank engine, suggested that it might like to work turn and turn about between Brighton and Rugby with one of the LNWR's 'Precursor' 4–4–0s.

So the famous trials of November 1909 came about. The chosen 'I3', No 23, was not fitted with a water scoop yet she

The celebrated 'I3' 4–4–2T No 23, star of the 1909 Brighton to Rugby runs, leaving Patcham Tunnel with an up train of assorted former LB & SCR non-corridors on 7 June 1933 (Madgwick Collection, Brighton Libraries).

Top *'I3' No 23 in charge of the 'Sunny South Express' made up of LNWR corridor stock approaching the end of its long run from Rugby to Brighton in October 1909 (Brighton Libraries).*

Above *The 'City Limited' in early Southern Railway days made up of Panter balloon-roofed stock hauled by 'H2' 'Atlantic' No B424 passing under overhead wires near New Cross Gate (Author's collection).*

never once ran dry over the 77.2 miles which she was asked to run non-stop between Willesden and Rugby with 250 tons at an average speed of around 53 mph. Moreover, the $3\frac{1}{4}$ tons of coal piled into her bunker before she left Brighton saw her all the way to Rugby and back again.

The LNWR, and the rest of the railway world, was astonished. Superheating was then virtually untried, but immediately Bowen-Cooke, the Crewe CME, began work on a superheated version of the 'Precursor', which was to become the excellent 'George V' Class, and superheating was once and for all established as essential for practically all but shunting engines. Thus did the 'I3s' achieve fame.

I once thought I saw a ghost of an 'I3'. It was on a sunny spring morning in 1953 near Clapham Junction, not, I have to admit, a very likely setting for a supernatural vision. I had got to know the class well for they ended their days on the Oxted line and I often used to see them go by. With the advent of the Brighton-built LMS-type 2–6–4Ts in 1950–1 they were rapidly withdrawn and the last had been taken out of service in the spring of 1952. On the morning in question I had embarked on a trainspotting expedition to London. On popping my head out of the window of our 4SUB as we left Clapham Junction for Victoria, I saw heading rapidly towards me on the down fast line an 'I3', but I didn't have time to note its number before pulling my head back in order to avoid decapitation. It will be argued that the 'I3s', particularly when viewed head on, quite closely resembled other Brighton classes which were still around in 1953, and all sensible people will accept this as the explanation. But they'll have to do better than that to convince me . . .

Marsh's carriages broke away from LB&SCR traditions, although they weren't really his at all, for A.H. Panter was appointed Carriage and Wagon Works Manager in 1898. One of

Marsh 'J' Class 4–6–2T No 326 Bessborough *newly out-shopped from Brighton works in March 1912 (Author's collection).*

Bessborough *at the end of its days as British Railways No 32326 adorned in lined malachite green livery at New Cross shed shortly before withdrawal in June 1951. Behind is 'I3' No 2078, withdrawn in January 1951 (Author's collection).*

the reforms Marsh instituted at Brighton works was the complete separation of the Carriage and Wagon Department; in 1902 a new site was decided upon in the Brighton area alongside the coast line at Lancing. However, there can have been no great urgency, for some ten years passed before it was completed. A special train ran to and from Brighton for the workers which inevitably in later years was dubbed the 'Lancing Belle', though there was precious little resemblance between its ancient steam-hauled non-corridor carriages and the Pullmans found on the real 'belles'.

Panter was following in his father's footsteps, for Panter senior had been in charge of LSWR carriages from 1885 to 1905. Panter junior had worked both at Eastleigh and at the LNWR works at Wolverton. His new LB&SCR carriages had a totally different roof aspect. Gone was the previous almost flat profile, and instead the elliptical design which was becoming universal elsewhere was adopted. 'Embraced' rather than merely 'adopted' would perhaps be a better description, for so vast was it that it soon became known as the 'balloon' roof. The 'City Limited', the first-class-only businessmen's express which left Brighton at 8.45 am — senior city gents did not get to the office before 10 o'clock in those days — and returned from London Bridge at 5 pm, was given a set of these most handsomely appointed vehicles, some of which were actually gangwayed to each other and the Pullman. But this was an exception, and non-gangways remained the rule until the Grouping. 'Balloon' roofs appeared on all sorts of vehicles, including some rail-motor trailers which totally dwarfed the 'Terriers' providing the motive power, but the old, low profile was not abandoned and was used on all electric multiple-unit carriages.

Marsh retired in 1911. At the end of the previous year, an enlarged 'I3', the 'J1' Class outside-cylinder 4–6–2T No 325 *Abergavenny* had appeared, and work had started on a second engine, No 326 *Bessborough*, but this was postponed and did not appear until March 1912, by which time Marsh's successor had incorporated various modifications, principally Walschaert's as opposed to Stephenson's valve gear. Although not as economical as the 'I3s', the two handsome 'Pacific' tanks were fast and powerful, *Bessborough* having the edge over her sister.

150 YEARS OF THE BRIGHTON LINE

Left *Brighton station.*

Below *Stroudley 'Terrier' 0–6–0T No 55 Stepney of 1875 stands in front of the typically Wealden tile-hung station house at Sheffield Park.*

Right *A beautiful piece of* trompe l'oeil *restoration at the former LB & SCR station at Crystal Palace. The scene through the window and the door panelling are both carefully painted illusions.*

Below *The Underground in steam days – an Inner Circle train arrives at a station, possibly Bayswater (from a book given to my father when he was a boy at the turn of the century).*

Far right *Billinton 'E6' 0–6–2T No 32410 of 1905 at Norwood Junction shed in May 1956. (R.C.Riley)*

Below far right *L.B. Billinton 'K' Class 2–6–0 No 2346 in Southern Railway olive green livery in the late 1930s. (Colour Rail)*

Far left *'Brighton Belle' first class Pullman 'Audrey' as restored and running in the Venice Simplon Orient Express.*

Left *Semaphore days: a Class '73' electro-diesel at the approach to Bricklayers Arms, January 1970.*

Below *Where the LSWR and the LB & SCR met at Havant. A Saxby signal box protects the level crossing.*

Top right *A Victoria to Bognor Regis semi-fast made up of two 2BIL units and one 2HAL unit leaving South Croydon in February 1970.*

Middle right *The Selhurst triangle in 1973. In the foreground a Class '33' (Crompton) has charge of empty stock, in the scrap sidings are various withdrawn 4SUBs, including some 1925-built units, whilst in the distance a Brighton to Victoria express made up of a 4CIG and a 4BIG speeds past.*

Bottom right *The last 4–4–2 at work on British Railways, Brighton 'Atlantic' No 32424 Beachy Head, at Norwood Junction, 13 April 1958. (R.C.Riley)*

Top far right *Brighton-built preserved 'U' Class 2–6–0 No 31806 amongst the poppies of the 'Watercress Line' between Alresford and Ropley.*

Middle far right *The 'Brighton' lives on in the Isle of Wight. Preserved 'Terrier' No 8 Freshwater and an LB & SCR-designed non-corridor composite carriage at Haven Street.*

Bottom far right *The Quarry line on a November evening in 1987. In the foreground a Gatwick Express heads northwards, and beyond are the lights of Merstham station on the slow line through Redhill.*

Above *Terrier No 377S Brighton Works on an SLS special at Kemp Town, 23 June 1956.* (R.C.Riley)

Right *Brighton station with a 4EPB prominent in December 1987.*

THE END OF THE LB&SCR

Lawson Billinton, son of Robert Billinton, had begun his career under his father at Brighton works. He had worked his way through various departments and was a popular choice to succeed Marsh, who retired, in circumstances surrounded by some mystery, before he might have been expected to go and who subsequently lived on for a number of years in retirement.

With much of his period in office taken up by the First World War, Lawson Billinton was able to produce few new designs. He had, however, a most adventurous war, serving with the Royal Engineeers, being captured by Bolshevik Russians, escaping, receiving the CBE and ending the war with the rank of Lieutenant-Colonel.

Apart from the modified Marsh 'Pacific' tank *Bessborough* and the final ten 'I3' 4–4–2Ts which came out of Brighton works after he had taken charge, the first locomotives of Billinton's own design were ten modest replacements for the Stroudley 'E1' Class 0–6–0Ts. One wonders just why a new design was necessary, for although they were certainly more powerful than their predecessors, the old Stroudley engines soldiered on, gradually being withdrawn but still finding sufficient work for 27 of them to pass into British Railways ownership in 1948.

The original batch of 'E2s', as the Billinton engines were classed, appeared between June 1913 and November 1916 and was never added to. Some of the class were tried out on passenger work but proved unsatisfactory, and the ten spent virtually all of their careers shunting. They sometimes strayed off the Brighton section and although being heartily disliked at Hither Green were popular in Southampton Docks, which might mean that the former LSWR men were more open-minded and adaptable than the SECR ones — or it might not. A regular London haunt for the class was down in the yard at Battersea beside the power station and the former LB&SCR depot, and passengers on Victoria-bound suburban services could usually expect to see at least one at work there. After Battersea shed closed, the 'E2s' moved a few hundred yards under the former LSWR main line to the ex-SECR Stewarts Lane depot and carried on much as they had before, one of their regular jobs being empty stock on the Eastern side, which included the heavy Wagon-Lits sleepers of the Night Ferry. At

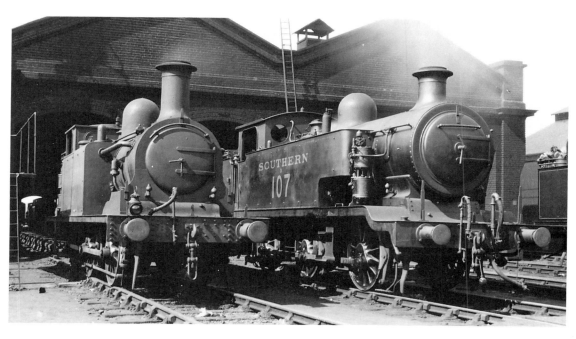

Two generations of 0–6–0Ts at New Cross shed in 1934. Stroudley 'E1' Class No B142 in March 1879 and withdrawn after a career of 71 years in October 1950, and Laurence Billinton 'E2' Class No B107 of 1913, withdrawn in 1961 (LPC).

Dover, other members of the class were similarly occupied, their compact size and considerable power making them ideal for such duties. Nevertheless, they were not a particularly well-known class of engine and it was rather surprising that in the 1970s Hornby chose to produce a model of an 'E2'; one would have thought a 'Terrier' would have been an infinitely better seller.

Billinton's second design was the 'K' Class 2–6–0, which fulfilled a need for a heavy goods engine which could accelerate quickly and keep out of the way of suburban passenger trains, and the first of the class, No 337, came out in September 1913. It bore a family likeness to the 'Atlantics', although the smaller driving wheels meant that the boiler was pitched lower and the chimney and dome were larger. Four more of the class were completed by November 1914, and by this time their great power was being put towards the war effort, hauling 1,000-ton goods trains and troop specials to Newhaven. Five more had been ordered in September 1914, but shortages meant that their completion was delayed until the latter part of 1916. A further seven appeared after the war. The class had charge of some of the heaviest goods duties on the Brighton line into the 1950s, and were also to be seen doing passenger work, although rather less frequently than the Maunsell 'Moguls' with which they were in many respects comparable, although vastly outnumbered.

And so we come to the last, and most spectacular, locomotive design of the LB&SCR. We have seen how the express passenger tank engine, of which the company made more use than anyone else, had progressed from 0–4–2T, through 0–6–2T to 4–4–2T and then 4–6–2T. The logical conclusion was a 'Baltic' tank, and thus the first Brighton 4–6–4T, No 327 *Charles C. Macrae*, was completed and began trials in March 1914. It might have been unique, for although a second engine was begun it was intended that it should be, for comparison, a 4–6–0, and a tender was built for it. At first No 327 performed excellently, so the second engine, No 328, was completed as a 4–6–4T. But then No 327 suffered several derailments and both locomotives were taken out of service while detailed consideration was given to converting them to tender engines. However, eventually various modifications were carried out involving the redistribution of the water in their vast tanks and the fitting of new bogies, front and rear. These did the trick and No 327 went back into regular service, followed by No 328, and gave no more trouble.

That the class had got over its teething troubles and was successful was shown by the building of five more after the war. The very last, No 333, was completed in April 1922 and named *Remembrance*, signifying that it was the LB&SCR's war memorial engine. In all, 5,635 employees of the LB&SCR had enlisted in the armed services, and of these 532 did not return.

The outbreak of the First World War immediately threw the LB&SCR into the front line supplying the horrendous war machine and its all-consuming demand for men and machines. To quote Jeffrey Richards and John M.MacKenzie in their *The*

The most successful of all the British 'Baltic' tanks were the seven L. Billinton engines of 1914-22. No 329 Stephenson, which entered service in October 1921, is seen when new in charge of a Brighton to Victoria Pullman express (Stent Collection, Brighton Libraries).

Railway Station, A Social History, when referring to the SECR, LB&SCR and LSWR, 'Troop trains and supply trains thundered over these systems day and night without cease'. The eastern side of Victoria was the principal arrival and departure point for leave trains to and from Dover. Some 19,740 special goods trains ran to and from Newhaven. Littlehampton handled 787,345 tons of war supplies, Newhaven 6,018,465 tons. The company's well-maintained fleet of heavy goods engines, headed by the new 'K' Class 2–6–0s, was stretched to its limits. They were helped out by Robinson-designed 2–8–0s of GCR origin built for the Railway Operating Department, most of which were shipped to France. Later, in 1917, twelve 'E4' Class tank engines were sent to work there; all came back in 1919.

Locomotives from many companies were seen in Brighton territory. GWR and LNWR goods locomotives regularly worked to Three Bridges, and Redhill was another important junction where trains from the Channel ports brought many foreign visitors.

Bombing raids, certainly compared to what would happen a generation later, were few and far between but, understandably perhaps, caused much panic, and the Brighton side of Victoria station was brought to a standstill for several hours one day in January 1916 when much of the English railway system seemed to be paralysed during a Zepplin raid in the Midlands.

A buffet for servicemen, organized and run by volunteers,

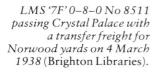
LMS '7F' 0–8–0 No 8511 passing Crystal Palace with a transfer freight for Norwood yards on 4 March 1938 (Brighton Libraries).

opened at Victoria in February 1915, and in the next 4½ years
served, without charge, some 12 million customers. There were
14 money exchange offices for troops returning with francs, and
other organizations in various ways looked after servicemen and
women going on leave. Brighton's Royal Pavilion became a
hospital for wounded soldiers and after the war an arch was
erected at the entrance to commemorate the men of the Indian
Army who had been treated there. A total of 233 ambulance
trains ran to Brighton in the years 1914–18.

Yet despite being in the midst of so much evidence of war —
and over much of the LB&SCR system there were times when the
guns could be heard firing on the Western Front — holidaymakers continued to flock to the Sussex coast and the Pullman
trains did better business than ever. A revolutionary step, a nod
in the direction of democracy and perhaps induced by war
conditions, was the introduction of third class Pullmans. They
appeared on the 'Southern Belle' and other services in 1915, and
although the carriages were conversions from elderly first class
vehicles, and were no longer dignified by names, being merely
entitled 'Third Class Car No . . . ' they proved very popular. The
last regular daily train on the LB&SCR for the exclusive use of
the first class passengers was the 'City Limited', and this finally
succumbed to third class invasion in 1921; to the surprise of a
number of its patrons, the City survived the trauma.

As the U-boat attacks on Allied shipping intensified and the
war dragged on, so home conditions worsened, although the
contrast between rich and poor was nowhere better seen than in
the hotels, boarding houses and tenements of Brighton, and at
the end of 1916 all Pullman services were withdrawn.

During the war the railways were under Government control
and there were many people at all levels both within and without
the industry, who felt that this situation should be regularized
and made permanent once the war was over. The Brighton Board
of Directors, along with those of most other companies, did not
share this view. In the event, as we all know, a half-way house of
four main Groups was decided upon, and thus the London,
Brighton & South Coast railway became, on 1 January 1923,
part of the Southern Railway. Brighton, along with Chatham,
was the only town, as opposed to a capital city, to feature in the
title of any of the most important of the 120 companies which
were amalgamated into the 'Big Four', and although it would no
longer be so distinguished, Brighton would continue to play a key
part in the story of the Southern Railway, and its successors the
Southern Region of British Railways and Network SouthEast
down to the present day.

THE SOUTHERN RAILWAY

At the end of the First World War the motor vehicle emerged as a real threat to practically every aspect of the railways business, competing for custom in the villages, elbowing its way into the lucrative seaside-bound day-tripper market, creaming off the former Pullman customer who could now purchase comfortable and totally reliable chauffeur-driven limousine, and offering an attractive alternative means of distribution for the manufacturers of everything from hazelwood sheep hurdles to mass-produced industrial products.

In Brighton, as in London, there were electric trams, and local services such as the Kemp Town branch felt the effects of this competition. Southdown Motor Services was formed in 1914, an amalgamation of a number of concerns which were already operating not just local services in the Brighton, Worthing and Lewes areas, but were also pioneering extended tours, one in 1913 being in a solid-tyred charabanc to the Lake District! After the war, Southdown expanded rapidly and began regular express services between London and Brighton. Brighton, naturally enough, was the goal for many charabanc operators and the canvas-roofed Leylands, Tilling-Stevens, ADCs and the like rapidly became a familiar sight on the A23 on summer weekends. They could not compete in speed with the railways, but they would pick you up at the end of your own road and, as the vehicles grew more sophisticated and reliable, the open-sided charabancs evolved into proper coaches (many of their bodies built by the Brighton firm of Harringtons), so their popularity was established.

The Southdown company continued to grow and between 1919 and 1939 took over some 50 other operators so that by the early 1930s it was the owner of a complex network of routes serving every corner of Sussex. All over Britain the railways were facing similar competition which they attempted to fight off in various ways. The Grouping gave them powers to operate their own bus and coach services, and in 1928 the Southern Railway decided to invest in Southdown, the result being that it became the joint property of the Southern Railway and the Tilling & British Automobile Traction Co Ltd. Tillings also owned the Brighton, Hove and District Omnibus Co Ltd, which, with the

Haywards Heath station forecourt with two Southdown Leyland Titan double-deckers dating from the 1930s.

The Palace Pier, Brighton, in the 1930s. Note the open-roofed charabanc (Author's collection).

Brighton station with awning, bike and buses, March 1988.

Brighton Corporation and Southdown, between them worked local services in Brighton.

As we have seen, the First World War brought to a halt the LB&SCR's electrification schemes. Raising sufficient money to continue them proved a problem after the war, and the impending amalgamation with the LSWR with its very different dc third rail system was a further complication. Nevertheless, electrification of the railways of south London and of the Brighton line was seen in all quarters as essential if they were to compete successfully with the road challenge. It is worth noting that the relief of unemployment was also put forward as a further reason for investing in electrification schemes; the promise of a land fit for heroes had turned sour within a year or so of the war ending, and many ex-servicemen found themselves without jobs. Some invested their gratuities in a motor vehicle, often a former military one which could be adapted either for passenger or for goods work, and although most of these small enterprises soon failed, some succeeded and provided competition for the railways from yet another quarter.

In April 1925, electric trains began to operate to Sutton and down the main Brighton line through East Croydon to Coulsdon. However, more than two years before, the newly formed Board of Directors of the Southern Railway had decided that the LSWR 600 volt dc system would become standard, and the Coulsdon and Sutton extensions were the last using the old Brighton company's overhead equipment. This differed from its predecessors in that bogie power vans were provided rather than multiple units; the power van was placed in the middle of the train, and the carriages were conversions from low-roofed steam stock, a number being fitted out as driving trailers.

This last ac overhead scheme was pure LB&SCR in all respects save one, and that was the livery of the carriages. The Chairman of the Southern Railway, Sir Herbert Walker, was an ex-LSWR man, and the new Chief Mechanical Engineer, R.E.L. Maunsell, was from the SECR, so there was not much likelihood of the Brighton way of doing things dominating the new company. In fact, umber was apparently considered as a colour for its coaching stock — the white upper panels had disappeared during the war — but the 'Parson's green' which appeared upon the LSWR electrics in 1915 was to become the standard Southern Railway colour. With chrome orange lining, black edging and black-shaded gold lettering and numerals, it was a most attractive livery, as anyone who has seen it on the superbly restored Maunsell carriages of the Bluebell Railway or the 3SUB motor car in the NRM at York will surely agree.

Passenger locomotives were painted in a similar shade of green, lined out in black and white with mid chrome yellow lettering and numerals; it too was a most handsome colour

The EMU sidings at Coulsdon North in September 1968: 4SUBs, a 6PAN and a 4EPB.

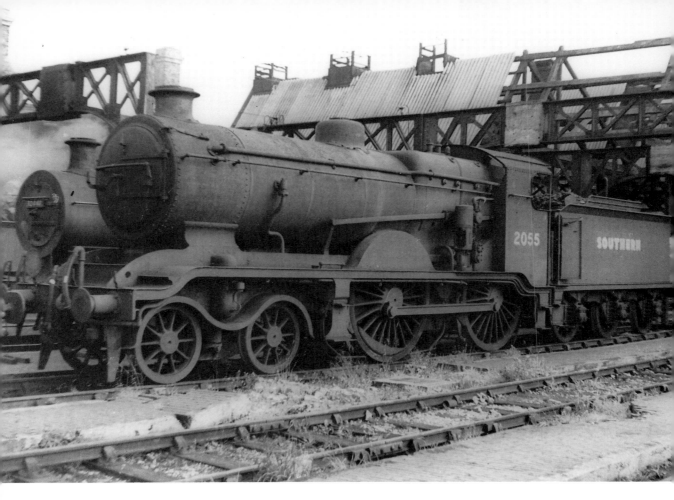

scheme and suited the former LB&SCR locomotives to which it was applied very well.

There was one class which never wore Brighton umber, and that was the 'B4X'. Billinton decided to fit 12 of his father's 'B4' express engines with 'K' Class boilers, but only two reappeared in their new form before the LB&SCR went out of existence. Despite this extensive rebuild, which included new frames, the old constricted front end was retained and the result was an engine which looked most impressive but was a sad disappointment. The 'B4Xs' were taken off top link duties as soon as possible and were banished to less demanding work on the Oxted line, with occasional forays on to the Eastern and Western Sections, which quickly sent them back. The last was withdrawn by December 1951.

Luckily, the rest of the locomotive stock which was passed to the Southern Railway was much better fitted for its duties and the 'Baltic', 'Pacific' and 'I3' tanks and the 'Atlantics' continued their good work on the main line which, despite the threat from the motor coach operators and the private car, was as busy as ever.

It might be as well at this point to explain that with the

formation of the Southern Railway, the former SECR lines became the Eastern section, those of the LB&SCR the Central section, and those of the LSWR the Western section. Former SECR engines had an 'A' for Ashford placed in front of their numbers, LB&SCR 'B' for Brighton, and LSWR 'E' for Eastleigh. Eventually these prefixes were dropped, and former LSWR numbers were left as they were, 1,000 was added to those of former SECR locomotives and 2,000 to all former LB&SCR locomotives.

In March 1926 the first of Maunsell's development of the LSWR 'N15' Class 4–6–0, the 'King Arthurs', reached the Brighton line. The final 14 of the class, Nos 793–806, were fitted with short, six-wheel tenders so that they could be accommodated on the ex-LB&SCR turntables.

Another Maunsell design to take up work on the Brighton line, and one more in line with its traditions, was the 'K' Class 2–6–4T. Nine of them, Nos A791–A799, were built by Armstrong Whitworth and entered service in the early summer of 1925, whilst a further ten were built in the following year at Brighton works and sent to work on the Eastern section.

The big tank engines, although quite fast and powerful, had barely enough water capacity to cope with the heavy Brighton line expresses and were transferred to the Eastern section when the 'King Arthurs' arrived. Shortly after this, their derailment troubles began, culminating in the Sevenoaks disaster in August 1927 which resulted in the conversion of the entire class, by then known as the 'Rivers', into tender engines.

The 'King Arthurs' did well enough on the Brighton line and they were certainly needed, for one of the first actions of the Southern Railway had been to introduce corridor carriages, which meant that the average weight of a Brighton express, with its Pullman, was now around 300 tons. However, the big Billinton and Marsh tank engines and the 'Atlantics' still handled many of the principal trains and it would only be electrification which would finally oust them.

No 4332, one of the
1925-built 3SUB units,
augmented with a post-war
Bulleid all-steel trailer,
stands at Coulsdon North in
February 1955 on a
Victoria working.

Empty stock from Crystal
Palace to Epsom Downs station hurries past Belmont on
Derby Day, 6 June, in the
Coronation year of 1953.
The leading unit is made up
of former LB & SCR motor
cars and former LSWR
trailers (Lens of Sutton).

One of the original LB &
SCR overhead electric units,
converted by the Southern
Railway to third rail operation, at Mitcham Junction
on 17 October 1954.

THE THIRD RAIL

T he Southern Railway got rid of the overhead AC system as soon as it could. The South London and Crystal Palace routes were converted to third rail in June 1928 and the very last overhead working was from Victoria to Coulsdon North just after midnight on Sunday 22 September 1929. The carriages were also converted, to three-car units which could work in pairs or, with two trailers in between, as eight-car trains at peak periods. They were joined by other units of SECR and LSWR origin, usually made up of vehicles which had started out as steam stock, although there were some built new as three-car EMUs by Maunsell in 1925.

With electrification proceeding apace all over the Southern's suburban routes, former Brighton units could just as easily find themselves working out of Cannon Street and Charing Cross to Greenwich, or from Waterloo on the Hounslow Loop, for example, as on home territory. However, the former South London line units, many with their flattened roofs over the guard's and driver's compartments where the pantographs had been fixed, continued in their original haunts and on the West Croydon to Wimbledon line, sections of which were, uniquely, single track and distinctly rural.

One might have thought that there would be nothing to do with the motor vans — which were in effect locomotives — but break them up. But they were only four years old and after sitting around for a while in Streatham Hill depot someone was struck with the idea that they might make excellent goods brake vans. And so they did. Stripped of all their electrical equipment and rebuilt to resemble the standard SR four-wheel van, their massive construction and bogie configuration ensured braking and riding characteristics of such quality that a number of similar vehicles were built new by the Southern Railway and are still in use today, making them almost the oldest vehicles of any description regularly at work on British Rail.

At the end of the 1920s, AEC and Leyland, the biggest commercial vehicle producers in the country, brought out their Regal and Regent, and Tiger and Titan motor coach and bus models respectively, which were a huge jump forward and greatly boosted sales; Southdown invested in a large fleet of

One of the Southern Railway goods bogie brakes based on the LB & SCR overhead electric motor vans at Lovers Walk sidings, Brighton, in August 1988. A 4CIG is crossing the Brighton Road viaduct in the background.

An elegant Southdown Leyland Tiger coach, built in 1936, parked in one of the Pimlico squares just behind Victoria railway and coach stations in the summer of 1955.

Leylands, adding to it every year until 1939. In 1931 the first Bedfords, cheap, reliable and seating fewer than 30 people, appeared and sold in their thousands to the small operator. Some 300,000 Austin Sevens were built between 1922 and 1940, the Morris 8 had sold half a million by 1938 and, together with Dagenham-built Fords, motor-cycle combinations and ever-increasing numbers of Standards, Hillmans, Vauxhalls and numerous other makes, were beginning to cause such congestion on the Brighton road at weekends that the hospital at Crawley had to be enlarged to cater for accident victims and the talk was all of by-passes and dual carriageways.

Despite the stock-market crash of 1929 and the consequent depression, most of southern England seemed hell-bent on getting itself to the seaside each weekend between the wars, and, if the Southern Railway was to retain its slice of the business and perhaps even increase it, electrification could be delayed no longer. On 21 February 1930 the company announced that it was to begin electrification of the London to Brighton and Worthing routes.

On the face of it, this was no especially big deal; it was only 35 miles from Coulsdon North, where the third rail then ended, to Brighton. But the Brighton line would be the first all-electric main line in the world, although this has to be qualified, for steam would still be in charge of goods traffic and through trains from other, non-electrified routes. Electric multiple units would handle all the passenger traffic. Immediately the cry went up from the regular patrons — 'What will happen to our Pullmans?' 'Fear not,' said the the Southern, 'we have been in full consultation with the Pullman Car Company and it is all settled.

The 'Brighton Belle' speeds along the Quarry line (Author's collection).

Thirty-eight brand-new all-metal Pullmans have been ordered from the Metropolitan Cammell Carriage & Wagon Co Ltd of Birmingham.' 'Of Birmingham?,' enquired the regular patrons. 'Of Birmingham,' replied the Southern. 'A highly-experienced firm which has been building Pullmans and other carriages for railways all over the world for many years.' 'Excellent,' said the regular patrons.

Fifteen of the Pullmans would be formed into five-car units for the 'Southern Belle', making this the first multiple-unit Pullman train in the world. The rest would go singly into six-car express units, the other five vehicles of each unit being of Southern Railway design.

The work began, and by 17 July 1932 electric trains were running as far south as Three Bridges, comprising four-car units designed to handle all the semi-fast and stopping services. In general appointments and appearance they closely resembled contemporary Southern Railway steam stock. There was an all-third motor coach at each end containing the guard's section and driving cab, and two trailer composites. Of the four carriages, only one of the trailer composites had a corridor, with a lavatory at each end, so that essentially the units were of compartment layout and only suitable for fairly short journeys. They were classified 4LAVs, even though they had only two, but for all their shortcomings they were amongst the most comfortable of the first generation of electric multiple units. Some of their first class compartments were in later days downgraded to second; when I was working on late turn at Gatwick Airport station in 1962 I often used to return home in a 4LAV and would make sure I got into a former first class compartment. It had deep, comfortable cushions and bags of leg room, and even though the carriages were 30 years old they afforded a highly civilized mode of travel.

The first of January 1933 was the great day when the electrics

Two 4LAV units, No 2924 leading, on a Brighton to Victoria stopping train near Hassocks in August 1967.

officially got to Brighton. Of course there had been trial runs before this, and on the last day of the old year the *Sussex Daily News* featured a full page spread of the inaugural ceremonial run from Victoria to Worthing and Brighton. The Lord Mayor of London, Alderman Sir Percy Greenaway, was pictured being welcomed at Worthing in front of what looks like unit No 2023 by the town's mayor on what was obviously a very wet day, whilst a further picture showed a ceremonial group including the Mayor of Brighton on Brighton station. Behind the group is what is either Stephenson's *Rocket* or a full-sized replica of it, although there is not a word of explanation as to how this got there nor how it was taken away again.

Neither did the *Daily News* consider it worth reporting any of the speeches which presumably were made. However, there was quite a lot about the new electrics in the news and correspondence pages during the subsequent week. Alfred Keeping of Pope's Folly, Brighton (what an interesting address, presumably not unconnected with the Lewes fifth of November celebrations and the Protestant martyrs), wrote regretting the passing of the Kemp Town motor train. 'The company have never done anything to popularise the Kemp Town branch . . . yet they still keep open the Dyke line where, in comparison, no one wants to go,' he complained. Whether Mr Keeping felt vindicated when this latter branch, which left the coast line at Aldrington halt west of Hove station, closed on the last day of December 1938 is not recorded. 'A miniature though standard-gauge mountain railway rising from the coast into the heart of the South Downs' was how the *Railway Magazine* described it. Once very popular with visitors to the Downs and to the amazing aerial ropeway which spanned the great cleft alleged to have been created by the Devil, it could not compete with the more direct motorbus services.

A couple of days later another letter from Mr Keeping noted that apart from the preserved *Gladstone*, the only engine of this

6PAN express unit No 3025 coupled to a 6PUL unit speeds along the main line with a Victoria to Worthing and Littlehampton working in the summer of 1937 (Author's collection).

famous class still in existence was No 172 *Littlehampton*. *Littlehampton* was withdrawn later that year, in September, but the preservation of *Gladstone* was a most notable event and worth recalling. It had last run in December 1926 and the Stephenson Locomotive Society, which had long been active in Brighton, was concerned that such a famous engine might be broken up. The Southern Railway agreed that if the Society would pay for its restoration it would be given to them. The work was carried out in Brighton works, on very generous terms, and after being exhibited in various places, *Gladstone* went to York Museum, where it can be seen today. It has returned to Brighton metals just once, in 1982, when the Bluebell Railway had it on display, although not in steam, during its centenary year celebrations. *Gladstone* was the first locomotive to be preserved by a group of enthusiasts — the first of many, as it was to turn out.

On 7 January the *Daily News* arranged for 'Old Wally', who had worked on the railway for 47 years, the last four as guard on the Kemp Town motor, to take a ride in one of the new electrics. ' "My! but that's wonderful," were his final words as the train slid quietly out of the station with quick acceleration.'

One of the most remarkable aspects of the new timetable was that despite the 'quick acceleration' of the electric trains, the overall time for the non-stop run between London and Brighton remained at 60 minutes. The philosophy of Sir Herbert Walker, the powerful and much respected Chairman of the Southern Railway, was that its electrified services should primarily be frequent, reliable and comfortable rather than particularly fast. He had sound commercial backing for this, and certainly on the

Brighton line traffic increased by 29 per cent in the first year of electrification, whilst throughout the network the total passenger mileage rose from 40 million in 1923 to 60 million in 1938. This was entirely due to electrification and the encouragement it gave to regular travellers to buy season tickets.

On that first day of operation, the new electric 'Southern Belle' also caused a great stir. Cheeering crowds watched the first all-electric Pullman multiple-unit express in the world begin its first scheduled run at 11 am. *En route* the passengers were regaled with melodic renderings from the London Madrigal Group, everyone remarking on the excellent acoustics of the carriages. More crowds lined the trackside all the way to Brighton, where yet more enthusiastic admirers awaited the train. One can excuse the eulogies of the press over the furnishings, for they really were rather sumptuous. There were etchings by James McBey and Sir D. Y. Cameron and veneers in woods 'from various parts of the Empire' panelling the carriage sides, whilst above the comfortable individual seats were set wall lights in the pattern of the rays of the setting sun, a motif redolent of the 1930s and repeated in the air-conditioning vents in the first class cars (the names bestowed upon two carriages date them as precisely as their interiors: 'Doris', 'Hazel', 'Audrey', 'Vera', 'Gwen' and 'Mona').

The Pullman Car Company was very proud of the ventilation

'Brighton Belle' first class Pullman car 'Audrey'.

The interior of preserved 'Brighton Belle' Pullman 'Audrey', now part of the Venice Simplon Orient Express.

system of the 'Belle' which was controlled by photo-electric cells and rejected smoke from the many steam engines still likely to be encountered on any journey on the Brighton line in the early 1930s before it could penetrate the interiors. This was augmented by sliding vents in the upper windows, framed in brass which was always kept highly polished. The cars were basically of all-metal construction but the ceilings, like the interior walls, were of Insulwood and there was a faint suggestion of a clerestory, the centre section being slightly raised.

Some 18 months later it was decided to rename the train. On a summer day in 1934 the lady Mayor of Brighton performed the ceremony and thus the 'Brighton Belle' was born. The new name caught on instantly. Motor coaches, cafes, bungalows and young ladies hailing from the town called themselves 'Brighton Belle' and the free advertising must have been worth hundreds to the Southern Railway and Pullman Car companies.

Not all the electric trains, however, were as grand as the 'Brighton Belle'. Those that worked the stopping service along the coast were really no better than the steam trains they superseded, except for being rather cleaner, for as with so much of the London surburban network, carriages converted from former steam stock were used. In this case, fairly modern former LSWR compartment vehicles were formed into two-car units. They were known as 2NOLs on account of the fact that they had no lavatories.

The success of the Brighton electrification led to the Eastbourne and Hastings routes following suit in 1935. Once again,

One of the 2NOL units, converted from LSWR steam stock, on a Brighton to Seaford stopping train (Author's collection).

six-car express units were provided; however, they differed in several respects from the Brighton trains. Most importantly there were no Pullmans; instead, a pantry, or what we would today call a buffet car, 'a beautifully upholstered vehicle containing five first-class compartments with removable tables and a kitchen with two serving hatches', was provided. Eastbourne and Hastings passengers had long been accustomed to Pullman service, so what had they done to deserve this deprivation? In reality, they were still well catered for. The 6PUL and 6PAN units worked turn and turn about on the Brighton, Eastbourne and Hastings lines. When traffic was heavy, a Pullman and a pantry unit were usually coupled together, and although from the outside a pantry car looked like a standard Southern Railway vehicle, it was rather luxuriously appointed and its passengers were served by Pullman staff. The motor cars, with their open layout, were fitted with sliding vents in their windows, rather like those on Pullmans, and the trailer carriages incorporated the latest developments.

The two-car units built for the semi-fast and stopping services were a great improvement on the 2NOLs. They were brand new

Right *The interior of a 6PUL corridor third trailer.*

and consisted of two corridor carriages, each with a lavatory but no gangway connection between the two vehicles. The Southern Railway seemed to have a peculiar obsession with lavatories and these units, having two, were code named BILs or bi-lavatory. The motor coach also included the guard's van. They were a development of the 4LAVs and were soon to be seen on all long-distance semi-fast and slow workings in Sussex, being built in considerable numbers between 1935 and 1938.

The Newhaven and Seaford branch was also electrified, as was the branch from Haywards Heath to Horsted Keynes. Of course, everyone wanted their own bit of railway electrified, if it wasn't already, and there was much lobbying on behalf of the Oxted line. After all, the sleepy little junction of Horsted Keynes was now served by electric trains, so didn't it make sense to continue the third rail up to East Grinstead and on to Oxted and so back to the main line at South Croydon? The Southern Railway would not commit itself at this stage, but instead concentrated on reaching the Hampshire coast at Portsmouth, both via the LSWR route through Woking and Guildford and the former LB&SCR mid-Sussex line through Horsham.

By the summer of 1938, all the principal former LB&SCR main lines and a number of branches had been electrified. The entire coast line, from Portsmouth harbour to Ore, in the eastern suburbs of Hastings, was worked by electric trains, as were the Bognor Regis and Littlehampton branches.

A quite different approach was taken with the final Southern Railway express multiple units. They were each of four cars, with gangway connections between each unit. The motor cars, as with the Brighton and Eastbourne units, were of open layout, while the trailers were side corridor. No Pullman cars were incorporated in them; instead, those for the former LSWR route had restaurant cars, those for the mid-Sussex line had buffet cars. These latter were designed by Bulleid, who took over from Maunsell in 1938, and although of traditional Maunsell appearance externally, had startling and attractive avant-garde interiors.

Although the 6 PULs and 6 PANs worked the great majority of scheduled express services on the London to Brighton line and the 4LAVs were usually to be found on the slow and semi-fast workings, such were the demands of this, the busiest of all the electrified routes, that any type of EMU could be found during the rush hour and at peak holiday periods. I was deeply disappointed on making my first excursion beyond the suburban area to find myself travelling not in one of the lordly six-car PUL or PAN express units but in ancient and despised 3SUB which

West Worthing on Easter Monday, 17 April 1933. Two LSWR 3SUB units Nos 1212/1267 stand alongside former LSWR Drummond 'T9' Class 4–4–0 No 336 in charge of the 3.54 pm Brighton to Cardiff train (Madgwick Collection, Brighton Libraries).

was what I was used to anyway! To this day, suburban units often work down to the coast, although in the case of the Class '455s' this is no hardship, for they are more modern than any of the express units and in some respects more comfortable.

Brighton has always been the most cosmopolitan of our seaside resorts. The vast proportion of those brought down for a day at the seaside by the new electric trains in the later 1930s were decent, law-abiding citizens intent only on enjoying themselves. But from the earliest days there has been a disreputable element attracted to the town by the rich pickings offered by the careless, the naive, the noisily-rich-for-a-day, and in the period immediately before the Second World War there were some vicious incidents involving gangs on their way to or from Brighton races. Out of this period in Brighton's history came one of the great novels of the twentieth century, Graham Greene's *Brighton Rock*.

Published in 1938 it tells the story of a doomed teenage gang leader, Pinkie, and Rose, the innocent waitress he marries in order to prevent her from giving evidence against him. The story is rich with the sort of characters one can still meet in Brighton today, and the railway also plays its part as the story moves remorselessly on. It begins as the crowds arrive; they came 'by train from Victoria every five minutes, rocked down Queen's Road on the tops of the little local trams, stepped off in bewildering multitudes into fresh and glittering air'. Later on more crowded in for the races: 'It was like Bank Holiday all over again, except that these people didn't spend their money; they harboured it. By eleven o'clock it was impossible to get a seat on buses going out to the course.'

Brighton Rock gives glimpses of a Brighton which was not only violent but where, behind the glitter and the bank holiday frivolity, lives could, as in much of Britain in the depressed 'thirties, be endured in deep, hopeless poverty. Rose lived behind the station off 'an awful little passage which stank like a lavatory', her parents' apartment has 'only one door and a staircase matted with old newspapers'. Although hardly more than a hundred yards apart, the worlds of those who sat in the beautiful umber and cream Pullmans waiting to leave for the West End and those of Rose in the slums down the hill from the station might have occupied different planets for all the knowledge and understanding they had of each other.

THE 1930S

And what of the locomotives and carriages displaced from the Brighton line by electrification? Swept away like the empty Woodbine packets on Brighton beach no doubt. Well, not really. For one thing, the Southern Railway, with electrification its priority, had built proportionally far fewer steam locomotives than the other main-line companies. Goods traffic was unaffected by electrification and the 'K' Class 2–6–0s and the 'C2X' 0–6–0s continued to handle the bulk of it. Older passenger locomotives, such as the 'Gladstones', disappeared, but the first of these had in any case been withdrawn long ago.

The chief casualties were the 'B2' 4–4–0s, the 'Baltic' tanks and the 'King Arthurs', and of these three classes only the former was actually withdrawn. The very last steam-hauled 'Southern Belle' had been in charge of a 4–6–4T, but with electrification these handsome engines were distinctly underemployed. Like a number of Brighton engines, their cabs and boiler mountings had been cut down to enable them to run within the less generous former LSWR loading gauge, and in 1934–5 the entire class was despatched to Eastleigh Works to be converted to 4–6–0s. This made sense, although there was an irony in it for it may be recalled that it had originally been intended that the second engine should be built as a 4–6–0. Reclassified 'N15X', the seven engines never seemed to reproduce the sparkle on the Western section that they had shown as tank engines on the Brighton line. Nevertheless, they lasted for some 20 more years. *Remembrance* was withdrawn at Brighton in April 1956, one set of her nameplates and war memorial plaque being put on display in the works. The very last, No 32331 *Beattie*, was broken up in the summer of 1957.

The 'King Arthurs' were not, of course, withdrawn on electrification, but took themselves off to the Eastern and Western sections where they shared top link duties with their many brothers.

Scrapping of Billinton and Marsh bogie carriage stock began about this time. The last slip working on the Southern, on 30 April 1932, was for Forest Row at Three Bridges off the 5.20 pm Victoria to Eastbourne express. LB&SCR corridor carriages being virtually non-existent, Maunsell corridor stock had taken

A delightful period piece from the mid-1930s at the level crossing west of Worthing station (Madgwick Collection, Brighton Libraries).

Norwood Junction shed on 16 June 1961 with 'K' and 'N' Class 2–6–0s, 'C2X' 0–6–0s, 'W' Class 2–6–4Ts and diesel-electric shunters in residence.

Former LSWR 'T9' Class
4–4–0 No 704 at Goring
with a troop special
(Madgwick Collection,
Brighton Libraries).

over all the principal main-line workings on the Brighton line
some time before electrification, but one could be sure of seeing
arc-roofed Billinton carriages well into British Railways days in
EMUs in the London suburban area and on push-pull workings
almost anywhere on the Southern Region. The balloon-roofed
Marsh carriages had a shorter life and none survived very long
after the end of the Second World War. The last former
LB&SCR carriages to remain in passenger service were across the
water on the Isle of Wight where they remained until the end of
steam in 1966. By this late date, preservationists were beginning
to appreciate that historic carriages were of equal importance to
locomotives, and thus the only three ordinary LB&SCR carriages
to have survived can be found, still carrying passengers, at work
on the Isle of Wight Steam Railway between Haven Street and
Wootton.

Locomotive building did not entirely cease on the Southern
Railway in the 1930s, and a small class of engines, the
'W' 2–6–4Ts, came out in 1931–2. They made use of the side
tanks and some other parts of 15 of the 'River Class 2–6–4Ts,
and with their three-cylinder layout and big, flat-fronted aspect,
they bore a strong resemblance to the Maunsell three-cylinder
2–6–0s. Originally allocated to Battersea shed, they were later
associated with Norwood Junction and spent much of their time
on cross-London goods workings.

Battersea Depot was itself a victim of electrification. Situated on the south bank of the River Thames beneath the approach lines to Grosvenor Bridge and to the west of the original Brighton and SECR lines leading to Victoria station, Battersea Depot had long been one of the most important on the LB&SCR with an allocation of over 100 engines. Inevitably electrification of the suburban lines reduced the number of locomotives living there, and with the modernized former SECR Stewarts Lane depot only a few hundred yards away, the Southern Railway decided to close down Battersea Park depot in 1933, the last engines departing in the summer of 1934. The big roundhouse immediately to the east of the main line remained for many years; I used to look down on it, battered but still more or less intact, in the war years and imagined it had something to do with the power station close by, and even now most of the exterior wall survives, although a section of it blew down in the hurricane of October 1987. Some of the sidings beside it are still used by the engineering department and the depot itself is used by a scaffolding firm. On the Battersea Park side of the main-line arches, the depot site is partly occupied by motor coaches using Victoria Coach Station whilst on the rest there has just been erected a grandiose office building, seemingly clad in marble, the home of the *Observer* newspaper.

Opposite is a building which perfectly illustrates how a fairly short passage of time can totally change the public's perception of what is good architecture. When Battersea power station was erected in the late 1930s on the south bank of the river beside the approach to Victoria station, there were many who considered it an eyesore, a vast blot on the Thames skyline. Pevsner, for

LB & SCR-designed 1st/3rd composite carriage No 6349 built at Lancing in 1924, brought to the Isle of Wight in 1937 and now running on the Isle of Wight Steam Railway, Haven Street, August 1988.

instance, in his *Buildings of London* published in 1952, does not
mention it, despite it being far and away the largest and at that
date almost the most modern building in Battersea. Its proportions are enormous and its four great chimneys, two of them
added after the war, reach towards the sky on a scale one would
have thought utterly impossible to ignore. Giles Gilbert Scott, the
architect of the great Anglican cathedral at Liverpool, designed
the brick cladding covering the steel framework. Gradually, since
the 1960s, Battersea power station has come to be seen as a
landmark in the story of twentieth-century architecture. Therefore when advancing technology left it redundant in the 1970s
there was no question that so remarkable and, many now
considered, so magnificent a structure would be demolished.
After considerable debate, work started on converting it into a
vast entertainment centre, work which involved gutting almost
its entire interior and even removing much of the supporting
structure, whilst leaving Gilbert Scott's exterior, the control
console and other artefacts which had engineering and historical
interest. When finished, the transformed Battersea power station
promises to be a fitting successor to that wonder of the mid-
Victorian age, the Crystal Palace.

By a sad coincidence, just as Battersea power station was
coming into existence the Crystal Palace met its end. A strong
north-west wind was blowing on that night of 30 November
1936 and fanned a fire which had started in an office in the
Palace. Before long the fire spread out of control throughout the
length of the great building, consuming the vast amount of
combustible material it contained and melting the glass. Despite

*The remains of the
LB & SCR roundhouse of
Battersea Depot with the
power station beyond,
February 1988.*

A 4VEP on a Victoria to Brighton semi-fast working, diverted because of engineering works to former SECR tracks, climbing Grosvenor Bank and approaching Battersea power station on the opposite side of the river, September 1971.

the infinitely greater destruction wreaked upon this area of South London during the war which was shortly to follow, the destruction of the Crystal Palace has entered folklore and is remembered far more vividly; and not just by the generation which actually saw it. When I taught in a school at the bottom of South Norwood Hill in the late 1960s and early '70s, boys and girls whose parents had been born in Jamaica and Barbados would relate in graphic detail the great Crystal Palace fire.

It seemed like half the population of London found vantage points or actually came to Upper Norwood to watch. Public transport could barely cope, special trains ran, the firemen of the 89 engines which attended the blaze made the High Level station their base, whilst water seeping into the tunnel outside the Low Level station caused such damage that train services were disrupted for a year and a half.

The two towers at either end of the Palace survived but were eventually demolished, the grounds became derelict and overgrown during the war years, and even in the early 1950s when I used to go and watch a young John Surtees, Morgan three-wheelers and suchlike on the race track which was built after the war, one could still wander amongst the neglected statuary on the weed-infested terraces which had once led to the main entrance of the Palace. However, such a prime site so near the centre of London could not be ignored for ever, and for many years now it has been the home of the National Sports Centre.

THE SECOND WORLD WAR

As August 1939 wore on, few doubted that war was imminent. This didn't stop Brighton enjoying itself — who knew when the chance might present itself again? — and the day-trippers poured down Queen Street from the station as they had every August for 98 years. But behind the scenes, preparations were going ahead for what must surely come. Many were convinced that within a day or two of the declaration of war, London and other great cities would be devastated by air bombardment as portrayed in the chilling film *The Shape of Things to Come* based on H. G. Wells's 1933 novel and starring Ralph Richardson (who had once been a student at Brighton College of Art). When Neville Chamberlain broadcast to the nation on the morning of Sunday 3 September 1939 announcing that Hitler had ignored the British ultimatum not to invade Poland and that we were now at war, Brighton was already coping with the 'emergency'.

Below the headline in the *Brighton Evening Argus* 'The Ultimatum to Germany' was the following piece, headed 'Evacuation Continues':

'The great evacuation continued to-day. The first train load arrived at Brighton station punctually at 9.59 am. There were mothers with children under five years of age — babies in arms and little toddlers. In many cases, the mothers were carrying the baby of the family and little parcels in the same hand, while in the other they had a suitcase. From their shoulders hung other parcels, or a rucksack, and their gas-mask in its cardboard container.

'Clutching on to their coat or toddling along beside them were one and, as often as not, two children, too young to understand what it was all about, but reflecting nevertheless the somewhat strained and subdued expressions of their mothers.

'Quickly and without any fuss the children and their mothers left the train and lined up behind their party leaders. This was a job that took only a minute or two, and then, in orderly procession, they walked out of the station to the waiting buses in Queens road.

'On leaving the platform a request was made over the loud speaker for "those with nothing to do at the moment" to help carry the Londoners' luggage to the buses. Boy Scouts and others quickly answered the call.

'A mother with a baby in her arms and a little boy of between three

Evacuees boarding a train for Brighton in September 1939 (British Railways).

and four beside her, whose luggage was carried by an *Evening Argus* reporter said they assembled at 6.30 this morning.

' "We had a comfortable journey down," she said. "It took us exactly an hour. We are glad to get away from London. At one time many thought they would prefer to stay, but now that it has come to the point they are looking at it in a different light. Of course, I don't want to leave my husband but I felt I had to get the children to a safe place."

'There were some 500 women and children on the first train and they were taken by bus to St Luke's School, from where they were sent to billets in the surrounding district.

'All the arrangements were the same as those which had worked so smoothly the previous day. Other trains bringing school-children and mothers and young children were scheduled to arrive at intervals up to 4.24 pm. The total allocation of the day was again approximately 10,000.

'Expectant mothers were being brought from London by motor coach.'

The report goes on to describe further arrivals at Hove, and Brighton and Hove between them received 30,562 evacuees, more than anywhere else in the country. So vast was the exodus from London in those first three days of September that not only were the usual London termini used but a number of trains started from New Cross Gate and Clapham Junction. The children and mothers were brought to the stations by London Transport buses and trams, and Brighton Corporation and Brighton, Hove and District buses, mainly Tilling ST type

A Brighton Corporation tram climbs towards Seven Dials, passing over the west coast line with the engine shed and works in the background and Brighton racecourse on the horizon, in the summer of 1938 (Brighton Libraries).

double-deckers, met them at Brighton station. The two bus companies announced that because of the evacuation only a limited service would be available for the general public. (Perhaps they regretted having got rid of the trams, for the last one had run on 1 September, being replaced by trolleybuses. The *Evening Argus* said the trams were '10 to 15 years of age', which was a wild underestimate; more accurately it announced that they were on offer at £5 apiece and suggested they might make ideal cricket pavilions or summer houses.)

The first day of the evacuation saw 14 trains arrive at Brighton, beginning with one from Clapham Junction which pulled in 'at exactly one minute to ten' with 900 children. The *Evening Argus* reported that the departure was 'inclined to be a little strained' with 'a good deal of weeping, but fortunately the early cheerful atmosphere was soon restored once the train was on its way'. Teachers were in charge of each group, 'the children were provided with stamped post-cards on which to notify their parents on their arrival and of their new address' and the *Argus* reporter was 'assured that accommodation had been provided for every child'.

There were those who were quick off the mark in helping with (exploiting?) the situation, and Cobbs of London Road and Queens Road advertised directly above the account of the evacuation a 'National Emergency Offer' of 'complete stocks of bedsteads and bedding at considerably below normal prices'. M. Barnard of Ship Street was prepared to advance cash loans of '£10 and upwards', but the publicity department of the Southern Railway seemed quite oblivious to the fact that its trains were fully occupied in the evacuation and it filled the two columns alongside the evacuation account with an announcment of 'Attractive Excursions from Brighton every Sunday, Monday, and Wednesday until September 27th'. One could take an excursion to Clapham Junction (one wonders how many takers other than trainspotters there were) for 5/6d, Chessington South including admission to the Zoo cost 8/3d, whilst Lewes was 1/1d. However, few of these ever took place, for on Saturday 9 September 1939 a list of drastic nationwide reductions in rail services was announced.

The statement read as follows: 'To meet other national requirements the Southern Railway regrets that it will be necessary to curtail the suburban and main-line services very considerably throughout the day as from Monday next. Overcrowding may result, especially at the peak hours, but the loading of the trains will be watched and adjustments made wherever possible.' However, the Brighton line was not hit too severely, for the number of trains each weekday would be 41, more than three times the number of any other destination; Portsmouth was next with 12, Tunbridge Wells and Folkestone had eight each, Eastbourne and Hastings seven and Bournemouth six. The 'Brighton Belle' and other Pullman and restaurant car services were withdrawn and rail travel became distinctly miserable.

In the event, the anticipated holocaust did not descend from the skies, the evacuees drifted home, train services were restored to something close to pre-war normality and even the 'Brighton Belle' made a partial return, running twice a day with one five-car Pullman unit and a four-car Portsmouth corridor set.

Then, in May 1940, came Dunkirk. Dover was the principal port from which the evacuation fleet sailed and returned with the weary troops, but many others all along the Kent and Sussex coast, including Newhaven and Shoreham, were used. All four main-line companies provided carriages for the trains which were provided to take the troops to their various destinations, an enormous undertaking. To quote Bernard Darwin in his story of

Troops returning from the evacuation of Dunkirk, June 1940 (Author's collection).

the Southern Railway during the Second World War, *War on the Line*, 'Redhill was at the very heart of it'.

Redhill Depot normally provided motive power for the Tonbridge and Guildford lines rather than the main London to Brighton route. At the time of Dunkirk the former cross-country route became enormously important and over 80 per cent of the evacuation trains heading for south and south-west England passed through Redhill. 'Passed through' does not very accurately describe the situation, for every train had to pull in from the Kent Coast and come to a halt facing London; its engine would then uncouple whilst another backed on at the other end, and then off it would go again. The complications this involved in crossing the paths of the busy London to Brighton line may be imagined. Nevertheless, so efficient did everyone concerned become that the average time between arriving and departing was 4 minutes; the record was an astonishing 2 min 30 sec.

The not very large Redhill shed was sometimes stretched beyond its capacity. Almost all the engines bringing in the troop trains had to be coaled and watered; 300 tons of ashes accumulated, the water once ran out and Three Bridges was frequently called upon for assistance, while the staff at both sheds, and at Redhill station, did their valiant best. For the soldiers on the trains which stopped rather longer than 4 minutes, refreshments were provided and this involved much working beyond hours, voluntary efforts, and frantic negotiations with local bakers, grocers, and other suppliers of provisions.

Troops rescued from Dunkirk in June 1940 'somewhere in South London' heading for leave in a train of LMS stock (Author's collection).

Troops of the London Scottish regiment alighting from a train of LB & SCR-built balloon stock at Goring (Brighton Libraries).

In the evacuation of civilians from London in September 1939, and in the bringing home of the troops from Dunkirk, the Southern Railway, and the Brighton line in particular, had proved to a grateful government that they could cope in a highly efficient manner with sudden demands during an emergency. Now that France and the Channel coast were in the hands of the Germans they were going to be tested, not to provide a spectacular, one-off, all-out effort, but to serve the ordinary public and to continue to run services as close to the timetable as humanly possible regardless of what the Luftwaffe could inflict day after day and night after night for as long as might be necessary.

The Battle of Britain began officially on 8 August, but planes had bombed Sussex many times before that and on 10 June the coast line at Shoreham and near Newhaven had been bombed, a train being badly damaged in the latter incident, its driver killed and its guard injured. Although the initial raids were on aerodromes and radar installations, many of them in Sussex, it was when Hitler ordered the Luftwaffe to concentrate on London, in his rage at a lone RAF bomber raid on Berlin, that the railways really suffered. Waterloo and its approaches were the most frequently attacked, probably more by accident than design, but Victoria and London Bridge also suffered considerably. One might have expected the latter, being so close to the Pool of London and the docks, to have been a prime target, and certainly there were many serious incidents. The worst was four nights after Christmas 1940. On that terrible evening there were 640 separate incidents in London. A burning factory collapsed on to the approach roads to London Bridge, so many water mains were broken that the water supply ran dangerously low, and much of the station was destroyed, the offices of seven departments being wiped out. Yet, almost miraculously, trains kept running, one line through the station on the eastern side to Charing Cross and Cannon Street remained usable, and there was not a single casualty amongst staff and passengers.

Earlier in the month a high-explosive parachute mine had floated down and the strings of the parachute had wrapped themselves around one of the London Bridge signal boxes. The stationmaster had ordered the complete evacuation of the station, but notwithstanding two signalmen in the box remained on duty for an hour whilst the bomb hung outside. At daylight the next morning, a young naval officer came down the platforms, and having left a written account of how he intended to defuse the bomb so that there would be a record if it went wrong, he was able to render it harmless.

Gradually the raids lessened in the new year, although as late as 17 April 1941 Holborn Viaduct, Waterloo, Charing Cross, Victoria and London Bridge were all out of use, and Victoria and London Bridge were hit again on 11 May. The damage to Victoria, particularly on the Brighton side, was soon repaired, but London Bridge looked a sorry sight for many years and it was decades before it was totally restored.

Only weeks before the Normandy invasion, the civilian population of south-east England, which had thought and hoped that the bombing raids it had endured in 1940 and 1941 were fading memories, found themselves under attack once again. Croydon suffered 1,171 raids, more than anywhere else in inner or outer London, during the war, and was particularly hard hit by the flying bombs and the later V2 guided missiles. The dense network of railways in Croydon was not too badly affected, the worst incident probably being the bombing of West Croydon station.

In central London the most serious raid occurred at 2 o'clock on the morning of 12 June 1944 when a V1 fell on the general offices at Victoria station; 17 people were killed and 30 injured. Of the 17 dead, six were Southern railwaymen, outside porters who were working as fire guards. Later in the year, at around lunchtime on 25 November, a V2 exploded on Woolworths at New Cross, just up the road from New Cross Gate station. The death toll was horrendous, for not only was a V2 loaded with high explosive, but being the world's first successful guided missile it flew so high and so fast that it could not be caught by aircraft and was seldom detected. It simply fell out of the sky without warning. Amongst the casualties were assumed to be two women carriage cleaners who it was believed had gone to Woolworths for their dinner and were never seen again together with two other staff at the station.

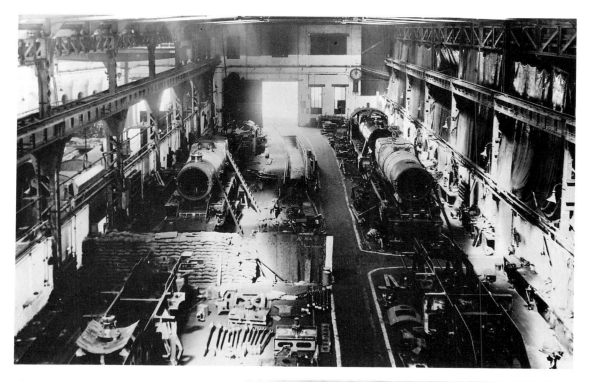

THE 1940S

One of the most dramatic effects of the Second World War on Brighton and its railways was the revival of the former LB&SCR works. Every little workshop or factory throughout the land, however badly it had languished through the impoverished 1930s, now found itself of vital importance.

Brighton Works had suffered relatively little from enemy action during the war. The worst incident was when a high explosive bomb did a fair amount of damage in May 1942, but normal working was able to resume within 24 hours. The most serious raid on the railway in Brighton was on 25 May 1943 when five bombs fell just outside the station. One Pullman employee at the Preston Park works was killed, five Pullmans and 43 electric multiple unit carriages at Lovers Walk sidings were damaged and an arch of the London Road Viaduct was demolished leaving the track suspended over the gap.

One of the discomforts of wartime travel was the blackout. Initially blue bulbs were tried out in carriages; they gave a miserable light, but despite that thousands were stolen. Eventually all carriages were fitted with blinds which had to be pulled down at dusk. Many of these with their notches cut into the wooden window-frames survived for some years after the war, but the crude black-out paint which was applied to some 300,000 carriage windows between October 1939 and September 1944 was scraped off as soon as possible. It was a tedious job — each window took ten minutes to clean with a razor blade.

With many men away, the Southern Railway took on far more women than it had ever previously employed. They did all sorts of jobs they had never tackled before, working in signal boxes, cleaning engines, collecting tickets and tackling heavy engineering in the works at Brighton and Lancing, for example.

In 1939 Brighton works employed a mere 253 men, but by the end of 1943 there were 755 men and 214 women in full-time employment there and another 38 women working part-time. Lancing Works was also busy and one task it was given was the conversion of 27 vans and three restaurant cars for Casualty Evacuation Trains, although they were thankfully never needed. Much specific war work was done at both Brighton and Lancing, as in the First World War, but there was also a resurgence of

LMS Stanier-designed '8F' 2–8–0s under construction at Brighton Works during the Second World War.

LMS '8F' 2–8–0 No 8168 heading through Coulsdon North with a Willesden-Three Bridges freight on 14 August 1947 (Author's collection).

*'Who's a pretty boy then?'
'Q1' 0–6–0 No 33028 hard-
ly adds to the beauty of the
Kent countryside as it
shunts a Tonbridge-bound
pick-up goods at Sevenoaks
on 29 September 1956.*

railway work at the former. This did not consist merely of repairs
—for the first time since the early 1920s, locomotives were once
again built at Brighton.

First came Bulleid's extraordinary-looking 'Q1' 0–6–0s. Bulleid never produced anything which looked much like anything
that had gone before, so the official reason that war restrictions
caused the peculiar outline of the 40 0–6–0s Brighton works built
in 1942 may or possibly may not have been true. Certainly no
one suggested that wartime shortages had forced him to introduce a new numbering scheme. The 'Q1s' were numbered
C1–C40. It was just as well that Brighton had given up painting
its engines bright yellow several decades earlier, for a 'Q1' so
attired would surely have born an uncomfortable resemblance to
a certain class of Brighton lady who adorns herself on the
principle that subtlety seldom gets one anywhere on a Bank
Holiday Monday . . . All their lives the 'Q1s' were plain black,
and they got on with hauling as many wagons as the operating
department cared to tie behind them. They were the most
powerful and the last design of 0–6–0 in Britain. The first, No C1
(BR 33001) is preserved in running order on the Bluebell
Railway.

The 'Q1s' certainly put Brighton works back on the map. But
this was only a prelude to full-scale production of 'Pacifics' for
express passenger work. The first of the 'West Country' Class
emerged in 1945 and, when production ended in 1951, Brighton
had built all but six of what proved to be the most numerous class
of 'Pacific' in these islands. There were 110 of them, including

those named after places, people and squadrons associated with the Battle of Britain. Again, Bulleid used his own unique numbering system; the class began with No 21C101 *Exeter* and ended with No 21C210 *66 Squadron*, or at least it would have done had Nationalization not intervened, for the later members of the class never received Bulleid numbers but reverted to orthodox practice and came out as Nos 34071–34110. No 21C156 received the name *Croydon* not only because the former London Airport became a Battle of Britain station but also in recognition of the great sacrifice the town had made during the Blitz and the flying bomb and V2 raids of 1944–5.

The 'West Country' and 'Battle of Britain' Classes were streamlined — Bulleid used the term, 'air-smoothed', but no one else could detect the difference. They were controversial engines both in appearance and performance. Personally, I thought they looked best in their original form in Southern Railway malachite green. They were a type of engine which needed a striking, rather than a dignified, livery and thus I never felt GWR green as applied in BR days did anything much for them. I recall my mother, who never took much interest in steam engines, remarking as we sat in our electric multiple unit in Brighton station one evening waiting to depart, 'What an ugly engine!', as a not very clean 'West Country' backed out past us.

But of course others felt quite differently, and readers can make up their own minds for a number of the class have been

Bulleid rebuilt 'Battle of Britain' Class 'Pacific' No 34056 Croydon *leaving Southampton with a Waterloo to Bournemouth express in January 1967. Not only was Croydon aerodrome, London's pre-war international airport, a Battle of Britain base, but the county borough was the most heavily bombed area in Britain, suffering particularly from the VI and V2 flying bombs and missiles of 1944-45.*

preserved, including No 21C123 *Blackmoor Vale* in Southern Railway malachite green on the Bluebell Railway and No 34092 *City of Wells* in BR green on the Keighley and Worth Valley Railway, whence she regularly ventures out to perform with great distinction on BR metals.

Bulleid not only managed to introduce new locomotives during the war but also brought out a new breed of suburban multiple unit. The first, 4SUB No 4101, appeared in late 1941. Its front end was almost identical to a 2HAL, but the body sides curved gently in order to make the maximum use of the loading gauge and Bulleid packed more passengers into his unit than had ever been possible before. They sat six-a-side in 11 compartments in the trailers, nine compartments in the motor coach. These conditions led to appalling discomfort and, following experience with the first ten units, the next batch, which didn't appear until after the war, had rather more civilized appointments. They also had a totally upright front with no curved dome, as had been standard on all Southern multiple units until then. Later, 4SUBs were laid out as saloons, although still with a door to each compartment.

In late 1951 the 4SUBs were succeeded by the 4EPBs. These in

A Victoria to Coulsdon North stopping train made up of two 4SUB units approaching its destination in 1973. The leading unit, No 4601, dates from 1950 and was withdrawn in June 1982. Disappearing into the distance on the far left is a 4EPB unit on the SECR's Tattenham Corner-Purley branch.

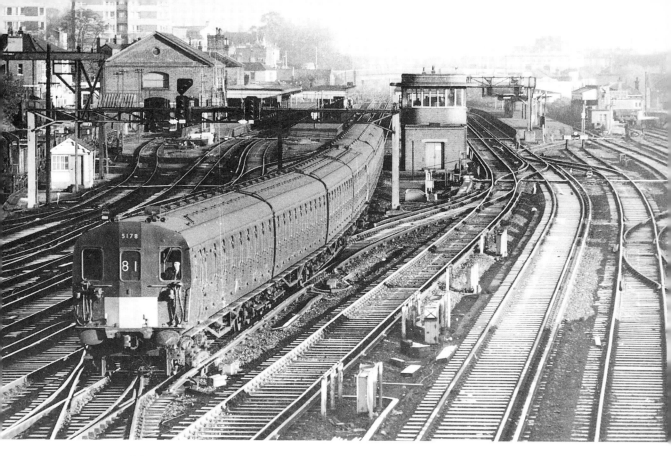

appearance and layout were similar to the SUBs — their doors, seats, etc were interchangeable — but their cab layout, control gear and electro-pneumatic brakes were quite different. The 4EPBs were unable to work with the 4 SUBs but they could work with all the units which succeeded them. Although Bulleid's 4SUBs have gone, many of his 4EPBs and 2EPBs can still be found on suburban services, on the Brighton main line and working services along the coast betweeen Brighton and Hastings. Internally they were not especially up-to-date when new, and today, with their vigorous ride and archaic layout, they have the air of dinosaurs from a long-vanished age.

Gradually the Brighton line recovered from the war. The old pre-Grouping suburban multiple units were steadily replaced by Bulleid stock, and later by BR standard all-steel sets, but they took a while to go. Those made up of former LB&SCR carriages were the longest-lived, and the last did not disappear until 1960.

A real landmark was the restoration of Pullmans in January 1946. Initially, the 'Brighton Belle' ran with one five-car Pullman unit coupled to a 6PUL unit, but on 6 October 1947 the full Pullman service was restored.

A vastly older electric service than that of the Brighton main line resumed operation in May 1948. This was Volk's seafront line.

Successors to the 4SUBs, two 4EPB units, both in original green livery, with No 5178 leading, pull out of Norwood Junction in January 1969 on a Charing Cross to Tattenham Corner and Caterham working.

SECR-built 'H' Class 0–4–4T No 1261 shunting Pullmans, the first one looking distinctly the worse for wear after standing out of use during the war years. Preston Park Works, 30 June 1947 (Brighton Libraries).

The first public demonstration in the world of an electric railway had been given in Berlin in 1879 by Werner von Siemens — it will be recalled that the pioneer LB&SCR overhead electrics used German equipment — and two years later the system was demonstrated at the Crystal Palace. The event attracted a great deal of attention, both amongst the public and the railway companies, and did much to bring about main-line electrification. The first tangible result was the Giant's Causeway line in Northern Ireland which opened in July 1883.

A month later, a ceremony inaugurated the first electric railway in England, along Brighton's seafront. Its creator, Magnus Volk, was a distinguished pioneer in the application of electricity. He invented the street fire alarm, in 1882 he brought the telephone to Brighton and in 1883, in his position as Electrical Engineer to the Corporation, he set up what was then the largest lighting system in the country and used it to illuminate the Royal Pavilion.

His railway was of 2 ft gauge and initially ran for a very short distance, a quarter of a mile in front of the Aquarium. The Mayor of Brighton performed the official opening on 3 August. The line, which used 50 volts, was later extended eastwards and converted to a gauge of 2 ft 8½ ins, the cars being adapted to the new width. Also a third rail was added, as previously the running lines had been used to convey and return the current. Ten years later, Magnus Volk unveiled a most remarkable electric railway in Brighton. It ran through the water. The car carried 150 passengers and looked more like a travelling pier than a tram, for it was equipped with lifebelts and a lifeboat. It ran on two pairs of tracks, was 24 ft high, and took its current from an overhead wire. It had a brief life, being dismantled in 1901, but it must surely have been the most unusual rail-borne transport yet seen in these islands.

Volk's more conventional railway is still with us, as are some of the original cars. Magnus Volk himself died in 1937, but he must have been delighted to have lived long enough to see main-line electrification reach Brighton. By the time his railway started up again after the Second World War it had carried some 30 million passengers, and it is so much a part of the Brighton scene that it tends to be taken for granted; it is easy to forget what a unique piece of living transport history it really is.

The Brighton line has had its share of serious accidents and just before the Southern Railway was absorbed into British Railways

Volks Railway. One of the 40-seat semi-open cars dating from 1892-1901 does good business as it heads towards the Palace Pier in July 1974.

the worst of all, in terms of casualties, took place on a foggy November morning at South Croydon. A bad accident had taken place not very far away at Stoat's Nest (Coulsdon North) in January 1910 when an up Brighton express hauled by 'Atlantic' No 41 was derailed, seven people were killed and 42 injured. No other train was involved at Stoat's Nest, but at South Croydon a suburban electric train, the 08.04 from Tattenham Corner, ran into the back of the electric 07.33 semi-fast from Haywards Heath to London Bridge.

Being the height of the rush hour there were getting on for 2,000 passengers aboard the two trains. The Tattenham Corner train was made up of pre-Grouping stock, the leading unit being ex-LB&SCR, whilst the Haywards Heath train consisted of 1932–built 4LAVs. The fog was dense, although it cleared later in the morning, and the Purley Oaks signalman was inexperienced. He momentarily forgot about the 07.33 which he had been holding at the signals, and although the next box up the line, South Croydon Junction, had just rung through to say it could now accept it and the train had begun to move, the 08.04 came through fairly fast on the same line and smashed into it. Both trains were badly damaged, particularly the leading wooden carriages of the former LB&SCR unit. Its driver and 31 passengers in the two trains were killed, whilst 58 were injured.

The grave of one of the October 1947 South Croydon accident victims in Coulsdon churchyard.

BRITISH RAILWAYS

The Southern Railway came to an end on 31 December 1947. It had a far shorter life than the LB&SCR, but in its 25 years it had transformed the Brighton line. Although from henceforth the line would be part of the Southern Region of the nationalized British Railways, for many years the change in ownership was barely detectable and as far as the general public was concerned the state of affairs arrived at in the late 1930s continued well into the 1960s. Elsewhere, new liveries, new policies, new trains, new forms of motive power marked a revolutionary break with the past, but the Brighton line had had its revolution and everyone else was simply catching up.

Just as former Great Western steam engines retained their original numbers on account of their brass numberplates which would have been very costly to replace, so presumably British Railways in the financially straitened early post-war years took a look at its newly acquired electric trains, noted that the vast

Early days of Nationalization. A scene at Longhedge, one of the many junctions between Clapham and Battersea where the former LB & SCR, LSWR, SECR and West London Extension Railway connect. A Great Eastern-built LNER Class 'J20' 0–6–0 No 4685 passes former LSWR 'M7' 0–4–4T No 676 on 2 September 1949 (Brighton Libraries).

The northbound 'Brighton Belle' with unit No 3052 leading near Patcham in September 1968. The front motor coach of this unit, No 88, is now preserved on the Swanage Railway where it makes its stately way through the Dorset countryside behind a variety of tank engines.

majority of them were painted green, and decided that for economy's sake the few which were not, on the London Midland and Eastern regions, should adopt Southern malachite green.

At least one 6PUL set had retained the elaborate lining of pre-war years throughout the war and into British Railways days. Inevitably this disappeared, Southern Railway insignia was replaced, first by the words 'British Railways' and then by the 'unicycling lion' emblem, but the Pullmans kept their elaborate livery, and as all the main-line express and semi-fast units and many of the slow ones were only just entering early middle age, the Brighton line carried on pretty much as before.

Brighton itself quickly recovered from the war years of neglect. Well, more or less. The more elegant of its two piers, the West, was beginning to show signs of wear and tear, but the Palace Pier with its variety of attractions continued to draw the crowds. Probably the highpoint of its career was when it starred, along with many of the most famous names in the British film business, in Richard Attenborough's satirical picture *Oh What a Lovely War!*

Brighton has always drawn the theatrical profession and many of them have lived in the town. The more successful in this precarious business regularly patronized the Pullmans, and great was the furore when British Railways announced that kippers were to be removed from the menu of the 9.25 am up 'Brighton

Belle'. They were put back but, truth to tell, British Railways had a pretty good case, for in an average month they sold only 44 breakfast kippers — or, to put it another way, 0.15 per carriage.

The Southdown company invested in a new fleet of motor coaches, although many of the pre-war vehicles continued at work throughout the 1950s, but there was sufficient business for all. All sorts of shortages, not least of petrol, restricted the private motor car, as Britain struggled to recover from the deprivations of the war. Many of these deprivations were beyond the immediate remedy of the new Labour Government, but, for all that, the late 1940s and early 50s were happy times when many were able to enjoy a relatively prosperous peace, the anticipation of which would have seemed unbearably optimistic when the evacuees were arriving at Brighton station in September 1939 or when the air raid warnings groaned out night after night over South London in 1940–41.

The new health service, secondary education for all and a huge slum clearance and re-housing programme, along with the virtual disappearance of that scourge of the 1930s, unemployment, promised a better world, and with money in their pockets day-trippers flocked to Brighton and the other Sussex resorts. Travel to the Continent had resumed and, with more and more

The pioneer Southern Railway electric locomotives at Three Bridges on 24 September 1946. CC2, on the left, waits in a siding whilst CC1 passes by on the 2.36 pm Norwood to Horsham goods (Madgwick Collection, Brighton Libraries).

young people going into further education, the Newhaven-Dieppe route, which was the cheapest of the cross-Channel services, became a favourite with students.

Electrification in the 1930s had been restricted to passenger services, but Bulleid had foreseen that one day steam would also be eliminated from goods services and he introduced three powerful main-line electric locomotives. They became a familiar sight on heavy Brighton line goods trains, but they also took over regular haulage of the Newhaven boat train. However, this often ran in several parts and when this happened the Brighton 'Atlantics' reappeared.

The 'H1s' disappeared early in British Railways days, as did one 'H2' and it looked as though these famous engines would soon be a memory. However, the five surviving 'H2s' were overhauled at Brighton and although they spent periods in store they also still performed well on a variety of tasks, ranging from the boat trains to the Brighton-Bournemouth expresses, inter-regional trains, Christmas parcels work, and, most commonly, on the Oxted line. The lined black which the 'Atlantics' wore in British Railways days may have been rather more sombre than Southern green, but it was always kept clean and did little to detract from the engines' fine proportions.

In the end, they were the last 'Atlantics' active in Great Britain and each month we would scan the withdrawal lists in the *Railway Magazine* to see how much longer they would last. Time caught up with them eventually and on a cloudless Sunday morning in the spring of 1958 I stood on the footbridge south of Norbury station and watched No 32424 *Beachy Head* steam past with a train of boat train stock from Victoria to Newhaven on her last run. Rumour had it that she accelerated so rapidly up Grosvenor bank that she received 'yellows' through Battersea Park as she was in danger of catching up with the preceding electric.

There were hopes that she might be preserved, but there was already a very similar Great Northern large-boilered 'Atlantic', No 251, as well as the original *Henry Oakley* in the National Collection, and it was not to be. And so the Brighton 'Atlantic' story ended — or so we all thought.

Many years later, someone discovered a GNR 'Atlantic' boiler still in existence, and what should the Bluebell Railway announce at the end of 1987 but that it was going to reconstruct a Brighton 'Atlantic' around it. Such a scheme would have been derided as totally madcap in the early days of preservation, but all sorts of extraordinary resurrections have been achieved of late. The purists will claim that it will be neither genuine nor even a totally exact replica. No one pretends that it will — mind you, most genuine elderly preserved locomotives are a bit like the broom which has had three handles and two heads during its career — but who cares? The Bluebell, having been in the business longer than anyone else, doesn't open its mouth until it knows there's a very good chance it can fulfil its promises. It may not happen until the next century, but I'll bet my first week's old-age pension that about the time I receive it *Beachy Head* will be steaming through Sussex once again and will smell, look and sound close enough to the original to bring tears of joy to a great many admirers of the finest of all Brighton tender engines.

Brighton 'Atlantic' No 32425 Trevose Head *passing Coulsdon North on a Christmas parcels train from Brighton to London Bridge on a bright cold December midday in 1954, a typical working for this class in its declining years. By this date the 'H2s' were the only 'Atlantics' at work on British Railways. In the distance, 4SUBs, mostly of pre-grouping origin, stand in the sidings. The non-electrified tracks in the left foreground lead to Hall and Co's quarry.*

EXPANSION AND CONTRACTION

O ne of the principal features of the slum clearance and bomb damage reparations in London in the years immediately after the Second World War was the creation of new towns. Just one was south of the Thames, at Crawley. Close by was a small aerodrome, Gatwick, which had been provided with a station by the Southern Railway in the 1930s, on the main Brighton line between Gatwick Racecourse and Three Bridges stations. There was some fear that this grass-runwayed airfield might be expanded into a full-scale international airport, particularly as the racecourse had not reopened after the war and its flat expanses invited development, but Crawley Development Corporation was assured by the government that this would never happen. Today Gatwick is the busiest single runway airport in the world.

The principal objection Crawley had to the expansion of Gatwick airport was on safety grounds; there have been accidents, the worst being that of an Afghan airliner which crashed on to a house in the countryside, but the airport has a pretty good safety record. It has certainly taken up much farmland, and the skies around are dominated by arriving and departing jets. But the other side of the coin is the huge number of jobs the airport has generated and the traffic which it has brought to the railway.

The main London to Brighton road, the A23, lay right across the expanding airport and was diverted eastwards. This brought it alongside the London to Brighton railway and it was here that the terminal buildings were erected, straddling both road and railway. Such an arrangement meant that Gatwick Airport had a transport infrastructure which no other airport in the country could equal. Most importantly, as far as our story is concerned, passengers could walk straight from a train to the check-in terminal. Heathrow could not possibly match this, the extension of the Piccadilly tube line being a very poor substitute for a proper railway.

A check-in terminal was opened above the platforms at Victoria and the 'new' Gatwick Airport station was opened on 28

May 1958. The 1935 Gatwick Airport station, ironically the newest on the line, was closed and the original platforms of the 1891 Racecourse station were used, but the rest was, to quote the July 1958 *Trains Illustrated*, 'handsomely contemporary'. Other features included two — yes, *two* — telephone kiosks and 'the forthcoming installation of apparatus to broadcast pre-recorded bilingual announcements'. Of course nothing dates faster than 'contemporary' architecture, but the 1958 Gatwick served its purpose.

A BAC111 of British United Airways coming in to land at Gatwick Airport over a mixed bag of BILs, HALs, CIGs and VEPs in June 1969.

An up Gatwick Airport to Victoria train on the Selhurst triangle in March 1970. The leading unit is one of the post-war 2HALs allocated to this service, next is a 2BIL, then a 2HAL, the two latter having come up from Bognor by way of the Mid-Sussex line.

In the summer of 1962 I had a holiday job working at Gatwick Airport station. The pre-recorded announcements were functioning by then and were certainly an improvement on the not always very clear diction of assorted porters, but we students — there were three of us — could hardly contain ourselves when the occasional working was due for which there was no tape and we could grab the microphone and broadcast to red-faced, sombrero-sporting customers suffering from jet lag and a surfeit of Benidorm chips and Chianti.

The post-war 2HAL units, which were a good deal more comfortable than their spartan pre-war ancestors, were rostered to work a half-hourly service between Victoria and Gatwick. The unit would arrive from London at the rear of a Bognor semi-fast, which would then head off towards Three Bridges and the wilds of the Mid-Sussex line leaving the HAL behind which would, in the fullness of time, return to London at the front of an up Bognor train. Of course, many other services, slow and semi-fast, stopped at Gatwick so that it had excellent links northwards to Redhill, East Croydon and London Bridge and southwards to most stations in Sussex.

Gatwick Airport seemed extremely busy in those days with its BAC 111s, Viscounts, Elizabethans, Britannias, 707s and occasional elderly Constellations and DC6s, but the buildings of the late 1950s would today hardly accommodate the cleaning ladies' mops. The station buildings have been totally rebuilt and greatly enlarged as the number of passengers using them has increased year by year. The destinations accessible by through trains and shown on the indicator in the vast concourse would have caused the hostesses, student porters and others of 30 years ago to rub their eyes in disbelief. And whereas the Pullmans which ran non-stop between London and Brighton were for so long the pride of the line, today the multiple units which have replaced them are very ordinary, and the mantle which the Pullmans wore has passed to the air-conditioned 'Gatwick Expresses', running every quarter of an hour during the day and every hour through the night between Victoria and Gatwick Airport.

In that summer of 1962, the electric scene on the Brighton line had changed little since nationalization, but steam, in 1948 still plentiful and much varied, was on its way out. Electric or diesel locomotives hauled nearly all the goods traffic and almost the only steam-worked passenger services were a few inter-regional summer specials in the charge of Maunsell 2–6–0s and Standard '4MT' Class 43–6–0s. Short-distance goods workings had declined drastically as the yards once associated with almost every suburban and country station and filled with coal and sundries wagons had declined, become uneconomic and had been shut. But to see what had happened to steam in the intervening years, we must return again to Brighton works.

The Southern Railway had built no passenger tank engines, apart from the short-lived 'Rivers', and LB&SCR-built tank engines still handled much of the traffic on the non-electrified routes, notably the Oxted line. So the Southern Region of British Railways gave Brighton the task of building a batch of LMS-designed 2–6–4Ts and these rapidly ousted the veterans. Their downfall was completed by a new design, the BR Standard 2–6–4Ts numbered in the 80000 series, which were designed and built at Brighton. The LMS-type engines were transferred elsewhere, and two have ended up in preservation in the most

Tunbridge Wells-shedded Standard 2–6–4T No 80017 passing Riddlesdown with the 07.59 Tunbridge Wells West to London Bridge on 7 July 1961. This was a most interesting working, the five BR standard non-corridor carriages being the only locomotive-hauled ones normally seen at a Southern Region London terminus at this time. They were provided to cope with the very heavy loading usually experienced on this businessmen's – and women's – train. The two Bulleid corridors were provided for first class passengers. With the withdrawal of the SECR birdcage sets, corridor stock became the norm for Oxted line services, apart from a handful of high-capacity SECR non-corridors retained for rush-hour strengthening. Dieselization saw this set transferred to the Western section for rush-hour Basingstoke-Waterloo workings.

'E5' Class 0–6–2T No 2594 crossing the River Ouse on the approach to Lewes with the 3.55 pm Oxted to Brighton on 31 August 1949. The birdcage sets lasted until the Hastings dieselization, and all had gone by the end of 1959 (C.C.B. Herbert).

picturesque of surroundings on the Lakeside and Haverthwaite Railway in Cumbria. For the remainder of the steam years on the former LB&SCR lines, the handsome Standard engines handled most of the passenger traffic and became particularly associated with the Oxted services.

The last-built member of the class No 80154, was completed on 26 March 1957 and was the very last engine built at Brighton works, which closed a little while later. Elsewhere, British Railways works would go on building steam engines for another three years, but before the very last, '9F' No 92220 *Evening Star*, emerged from Swindon, the preservation of a LB&SCR-built line and Brighton-built locomotives to run on it had not only been proposed but was about to come to fruition. We will look at the remarkable story of the Bluebell Railway in a later chapter, but first we must see out steam on the Central Section of the Southern Region of BR.

The Oxted line continued to provide a home for steam engines and locomotive-hauled carriages throughout the years of main-line electrification in the 1930s, through the war years, and into nationalization. There had been proposals to extend the third rail to Oxted and speculative builders had made a few modest incursions in and around the town in the hope that their investment would be rewarded, but nothing happened. The joint nature of the line also survived. SECR carriages, particularly 'birdcage' sets, made up many of the trains, and former SECR 4–4–0s and 'H' Class 0–4–4Ts shared the work with former Brighton and Southern Railway-built locomotives. After the slaughter of the early 1950s, the only former LB&SCR engines still with any sort of foothold were the 'Atlantics', the 'K' Class 2–6–0s and the 'C2X' 0–6–0s. There were plenty of radial tanks around Norwood Junction, Brighton and elsewhere, but they weren't much seen on the Oxted line. The lively little 'H' Class 0–4–4Ts more or less monopolized the Oxted to Tunbridge Wells West push-pulls into the 1960s, and the later rebuilt Wainwright and Maunsell inside-cylinder 4–4–0s put in appearances. That most common of wheel arrangements, the 4–6–0, had most remarkably never been seen on the Oxted line until a batch of the neat-looking Standard Class '4MTs' was allocated to Three Bridges.

Of course, the principal reason why the Oxted line was not electrified was that it did not carry sufficient traffic. By the late 1950s, the future of such lines was threatened by the notorious Beeching plan. I choose the adjective with care, for although some of the closures proposed and carried out by the Doctor were necessary, it is generally recognised that many others were a mistake and, indeed, in the last few years much effort by both preservation societies and latterly by British Rail itself has been expended in attempting to rectify some of them. Dr Beeching set about the task given him by the Conservative Government with such enthusiasm that not even his own station, Forest Row, was spared.

The first bit of the Oxted line to go was that between Lewes and East Grinstead. It first closed in June 1955, a legal technicality brought it back to life temporarily but it shut again in March 1958. The advent of diesel-electrics on the Tunbridge Wells Central to Hastings line in 1957 and electrification to the Kent coast from the summer of 1959 meant the transfer of fairly

'Schools' Class 4–4–0 No 30928 Stowe, *now preserved on the Bluebell Railway, stands at Sanderstead with the 4.40 pm London Bridge to Brighton via Uckfield in August 1961.* Stowe *was at this time shedded at Bricklayers Arms and 'Schools' Class engines were frequent performers on this train, although they were soon to be replaced by rebuilt Bulleid 'Pacifics'.*

modern carriages and locomotives to the Oxted line; Bulleid and BR standard corridors became commonplace and an immaculate rebuilt 'West Country' 'Pacific', No 34100 *Appledore*, was often to be seen on the 2.02 pm Brighton to Victoria in the weeks after it had had charge of the last steam-hauled 'Golden Arrow' in the summer of 1961. The very last appearance of an inside-cylinder 4–4–0 was by 'D1' No 31739 on the 4.40 pm London Bridge to Brighton in June 1961. The Schools Class 4–4–0s had a regular turn on a heavy morning up and evening down working from 1957, and were considered by many passengers as the stars of the Oxted line at that time.

Curiously, the one bit of the Oxted line, if we may define it as such, which had been electrified, from Horsted Keynes to Haywards Heath, was the next to go in 1963. Latterly worked as a single track with the other line used to store hundreds of withdrawn locomotive-hauled carriages, the section from Ardingly to Haywards Heath remains open for stone traffic. Then, in 1965, the Eridge to Hailsham line closed, which meant that this alternative route between London and Eastbourne no longer existed; the final section from Hailsham to Polegate closed in 1968. In 1967, the Three Bridges to East Grinstead (High level), Hartfield and Groombridge line went, so that all trains via Oxted to Tunbridge Wells, Lewes and Brighton had to go by way of Edenbridge and Hever.

Having got the bit between its teeth, British Rail next tried to get rid of the entire line from Hurst Green to Tunbridge Wells West, Eridge, Uckfield and Lewes. Thus the only bit to survive of the many routes which once made up the Oxted line would have been that from South Croydon through Oxted to East Grinstead, and none of the alternative routes between London and Brighton would remain. Permission for this wholesale closure was refused,

The last steam workings out of Brighton were in the winter of 1966-67 on the through Plymouth train when Brighton-built rebuilt Bulleid 'Pacifics' replaced diesel locomotives which were having problems providing adequate heating in the severe conditions. Brighton shed was by this date closed (the empty tracks of the depot can be seen on the left) and locomotives had to be provided from Fratton.

but the section south of Uckfield was allowed to go. This rather surprised BR, who had expected it to be the only section they would be told to keep open, and they had plans to build a new approach to Lewes across the water meadows of the Ouse. However, it was not to be, and the closure of the Uckfield to Lewes line in 1969 meant that another alternative London to Brighton route east of the main line had indeed vanished.

Meanwhile, to the west, the Shoreham to Horsham line closed in 1966, bringing to an end yet another London to Brighton route. However, it should be said in mitigation that no *electrified* line between London and Brighton has gone. The alternatives now, if the main line is blocked, are along the coast eastwards to Lewes and then via Plumpton to Keymer Junction, or westwards to Arundel and then up the Mid-Sussex line.

Not quite every passenger train on the main line in the first decade of nationalization was an EMU, and apart from inter-regional and goods trains there were a couple of remarkable survivors from long ago. One was the 5.25 pm from London Bridge to Reading and Tonbridge. This was a pure South Eastern Railway relic, and for some 25 years was the only regular steam-hauled rush-hour express to use the main line between a London terminus and Redhill. Well into BR days its carriages were of SECR and LSWR origin, although its motive power could be anything from an SECR 4–4–0 to a BR Standard 2–6–0. Another curious survival was an early morning train from London Bridge to Ramsgate which took the original SER route by way of East Croydon and Redhill. I travelled on it several times, usually behind a 'Schools' although on the last occasion we had a Derby-built Class '2' diesel-electric (later Class '24').

A 3H DEMU leaving East Grinstead for Victoria, seen from the derelict and soon-to-be-demolished High Level station in June 1970.

THE END OF THE OLD ORDER

For 30 years, the Brighton line had proceeded comfortably along its way, carrying passengers to the seaside, to the country and to work efficiently, cleanly and quite quickly in its green-painted electric multiple units. Freight was never the money spinner it had been elsewhere, but it had nevertheless been quite important and was dealt with by various pre- and post-Grouping tender and tank engines, the three main-line electric engines and, latterly, some diesel-electric shunters of both Southern Railway and BR design.

But throughout Britain, the 1960s was an era of change. The young were more affluent and independent than they had ever been, accepted values were being challenged, not least in the colleges and universities, and if Merseyside turned music inside out the new university on the eastern edges of Brighton at Falmer and the art college beside Old Steine were in the forefront of the revolution in intellectual values.

Pullmans, so long associated with the Brighton line, seemed to belong to an era and a way of life out of tune with the times. Privilege based on money, quite possibly unearned, had no place in a world where everyone deserved the best, or at least a chance to be helped up the ladder. If one tended to approve of all this but also thought Pullmans were rather special — even if one could rarely afford to travel in them — then one was in something of a dilemma.

It was not just the Pullmans which were out of fashion. The whole notion of 'crack' named expresses was frowned upon. As steam gave way to dieselization and electrification, it became possible to run practically all trains on any particular route at the same high speed. Thus many famous names disappeared, the 'Newhaven Continental Express' amongst them. It became an unnamed rake of blue and grey carriages hauled by an electric locomotive and eventually just one more multiple unit. Although a batch of Pullmans was built in 1960 by Metro-Cammell for the East Coast route, elsewhere Pullmans were being withdrawn and not replaced. In 1967, the 'Bournemouth Belle' disappeared,

more and more ordinary carriages were to be found on the
'Golden Arrow' until in the end sometimes there were no more
than three, repainted in corporate blue and grey and without
names, and finally this once splendid train — out of which we
porters might make the equivalent of a day's wages on a good run
— left Victoria for the last time on 30 September 1972.

And what of the Brighton line Pullmans? By 1963 they, and all
the 6PUL and 6PAN express units, had been in service for 30
years. Their riding qualities had never equalled those of
locomotive-hauled stock and the motor cars in particular were by
now really quite uncomfortable. The first British Railways-
designed express units, the CEPBs and BEPBs (the final B was
soon dropped), intended for the Kent coast electrification, had
appeared in 1956. They were four-car sets, similar in layout to

Left *A Class '73' electro-diesel heads the up Newhaven boat train north of Wivelsfield in July 1967.*

Below *A 12-coach Brighton to Victoria express headed by 4CIG No 7318 passes its withdrawn predecessors, 6PAN stock, at Hassocks in August 1967. The carriage on the far left is a first class pantry car.*

the Portsmouth and Bognor 4CORs, although of typical BR Mark I appearance. The prototypes, buffet units Nos 7001–2, and ordinary corridor units Nos 7101–4, were tried out on the Brighton line and remained there after the production vehicles emerged to take up their intended Kent Coast duties. They certainly rode better than the Southern Railway units, although not so well that it wasn't soon decided to fit them with improved Commonwealth bogies.

The end of the line for the 6PULs and PANs came in 1964, when the former North Eastern railway workshops at York were given the order to build 36 corridor (4CIG) and 18 buffet car (4BIG) units to replace them. Later there would be many more. The Pullmans would be withdrawn along with the other carriages, but the 'Brighton Belle' was not, for the moment, to go. The CIGs and BIGs resembled the CEPs and BEPs, but had smoothed-off edges and only one instead of two guard's and luggage vans per unit — which made sense, for six lots of luggage space in a twelve-car unit was a dreadful waste of seating capacity.

This time the new units really did ride very much more smoothly than their predecessors. Internally there was a feeling of lightness, but the external appearance was dated for, on other regions, Mark II vehicles were appearing on many of the principal services and soon air-conditioned stock would be in production. The CIGs and BIGs were painted in the traditional Southern green, although blue and grey was to be the livery of express stock elsewhere, with plain blue for other carriages, and it was an unhappy sign of the low status afforded Southern Region multiple units when both the Bournemouth units of 1967 and the repainted CEPs and BEPs appeared in dull, all-over blue. The CIGs and BIGs never suffered this indignity; when the first repaint was due they assumed Inter-City blue and grey, as eventually did all other BR-designed express units.

Not all the 6PUL and 6PAN vehicles were immediately withdrawn. A number of new 6COR sets were formed from them to make up a shortfall on the Kent coast lines. What the customers over there thought who had been used in steam days to much more modern and comfortable Bulleid stock may be imagined. The re-formed 6CORs remained in green livery with the exception of just one unit, No 3045, which was repainted blue. Its mixture of former 6PUL and 6PAN vehicles were the only Maunsell-designed carriages ever to run in ordinary service in this livery. All the re-formed units were withdrawn by the end of 1968.

By this time the faithful 4LAVs were also on the way out, to be

replaced by the 4VEPs. Introduced for the Bournemouth line slow services, they were pretty ordinary affairs, principally designed to accommodate as many passengers as possible, and although their riding qualities were improved, their seating and general appointments were inferior to the 4LAVs. However, they did have two advantages over their predecessors. One was that each carriage was gangway connected to its brother, the other that they could work in multiple with all other BR-built units. Unfortunately, this latter feature has seen their frequent use on fast services throughout their careers, an imposition which has not endeared them to the long-suffering public. None of the 4LAVs ever wore green livery, and just one acquired a bright yellow face. It ended its days at Polegate in 1970.

4COR No 3148 at the rear of a Brighton to Victoria semi-fast passing 2BIL No 2066 at the head of a Victoria to Bognor Regis stopping train via the Mid-Sussex line at Merstham in February 1969.

Mention of bright yellow brings us to the various experiments which went on in the 1960s to make both electric and diesel multiple units more visible to men working on the track. In the days of steam engines, billowing smoke and the noise of a locomotive working hard usually, although not always, provided ample warning. Presumably Brighton line gangers and linesmen had got used to the less visible electrics, but elsewhere on British Railways, with the disappearance of steam locomotives, problems arose and various stripes and yellow panels were tried out before a complete yellow front end was deemed the most satisfactory solution, all locomotives and multiple units eventually acquiring this feature. On the 'Brighton Belle', this meant the obliteration of the Pullman coat of arms beneath the route number at the front of the driver's cab, but a far more drastic change of livery was about to take place.

One day at the end of 1968, in Selhurst depot, I caught sight of a strange apparition. It was unit No 3052 all tarted up in blue and grey, the names of the individual cars and the Pullman insignia gone and replaced by the legend 'Brighton Belle' and the BR 'double arrow' symbol. It certainly looked different, and it didn't take me long to decide that I didn't much like it; but I supposed one good thing to be said for the change was that it ensured the survival of the 'Belle' for a while longer. All three units shortly acquired the new livery, along with roller blind number indicators instead of stencils. This feature was also extended to the

First class on the 'Brighton Belle' after repainting in blue and grey livery.

The down 'Brighton Belle' in the blue and grey livery approaching Patcham in the autumn of 1970.

4COR units, which still found plenty of work on the Brighton line, but not to the 2BILs and 2HALs, which were next in line for the breaker's yard once the 4LAVs had all gone.

It was shortly afterwards that I made my first and only journey in the cab of the 'Brighton Belle'. The long-standing 60-minute non-stop schedule had been cut to 55 minutes with the introduction of the CIGs and BIGs and the 'Belle' was also expected to keep to this. It had ample power, but the quality of ride was something else; the complaints had begun immediately after the war, a *Railway Gazette* reader in 1946 remarking that 'in excess of 45 mph reading is difficult and writing is impossible'.

An unofficial record of something under 45 minutes had been set by the 'Brighton Belle' some years before in somewhat unusual circumstances; one wonders whether any tea or coffee spent longer than a few seconds in their intended receptacles. Apparently what happened was that the 'Belle' had left Brighton a quarter of an hour late, and somewhere along the line the motorman realized he was behind schedule but forgot that he had started out that way and put his foot down. By the time he was sweeping through East Croydon at an unheard of rate, word had got to Victoria that something untoward was up and when the 'Belle' came to rest at Victoria in something under 45 minutes, a reception committee of shaken officials was on hand to 'greet' the errant motorman.

Nothing remotely dramatic took place on my run. We departed and arrived on time, a severe check through Clapham Junction and a lesser one near Patcham cutting our overall running time to not much over 50 minutes. I noted that 'We ran for a fair proportion of the journey with the controller shut and the old lady showed that as far as performance went age had no effect on her'. The cabs of the Southern Railway EMUs were pretty basic affairs, a cross between a lorry of the time and a tram – and there were plenty of tramway systems still in operation when the 'Brighton Belle' was built.

Diesels and electrics are often alleged to be soulless machines, each one absolutely identical in performance to its brother— although how any car owner can subscribe to such a theory is quite beyond me. Certainly electrics are far less spectacular than steam locomotives when on the move and are much more difficult — although not impossible — to photograph in such a way that their unique qualities of effortless, gliding speed come through. But electrics certainly do have their own special qualities, their peculiar and evocative noises, even their distinctive smells and, over the years, they quite certainly acquire personalities. Just talk to any of the members of the Southern Electric Group working away at the former Pullman works at Preston Park on the restoration of their 4COR unit. An electric, just like a steam engine, can even be coaxed into performing more or less satisfactorily when it is feeling several degress under. Hubert Hobden, a Burwash-born railwayman who began his career on the LB&SCR at Eastbourne shed in 1913 and ended it as a motorman in the 1950s, recounts a run with the 1.25 pm up 'Brighton Belle'. The signalman at Preston Park stopped him when he spotted flames. Motorman Hobden realized that there was a defect in the front bank of resistors, but calculated that he could keep going by driving in such a manner that they could be bypassed. There was a slack of 15 mph through Quarry Tunnel but by being re-routed through Redhill and thus having to avoid any sudden acceleration he managed to coax the 'Belle' to its destination, somewhat late but far better than having to fail her.

Despite the refurbishment of the 'Belle' and her excellent mechanical condition, her days were numbered. She was an expensive train to operate, and 14 Pullman company attendants were needed to staff her every time she ran as a ten-coach train — there was a pool of 36 in all. She took her place three times a day in each direction in the hourly fast service between Victoria and Brighton, and many of her passengers resented paying the 20p second class, 30p first class supplement demanded; all they wanted was a comfortable ride in an ordinary carriage, and they took no delight at all in the antiquarian splendours of the 'Belle' which so enthralled enthusiasts.

The end came on 30 April 1972. Since then, no Pullman car, let alone a complete train, has run regularly over the line with which for nearly a century Pullmans were more closely associated than any other. There was a private attempt with what was called

Brighton Museum in August 1988 showing the Pullman exhibition.

the 'Regency Belle', but it soon folded. The inaugural run of the Venice–Simplon–Orient Express Pullmans — one of which is the former 'Brighton Belle' car 'Audrey' — took place on 28 April 1982 between Victoria and Brighton, but usually the only sight the Brighton line gets of this magnificent train is as it pulls out of the Eastern side of Victoria station on its journey to Folkestone.

None of the 15 'Brighton Belle' Pullmans was scrapped. Such was their fame that they all passed into preservation in many different guises, ranging from static extensions of pubs to conversions to run behind steam locomotives. Three third class cars remain in Sussex, No 86 on the Bluebell Railway, and driving motor cars Nos 92 and 93 at the former Pullman works at Preston Park. The Bluebell also had a former 6PUL car, 'Bertha', restored and converted to steam haulage.

The withdrawal of the 'Belle' left a handful of 4CORs as the final representatives of the pre-war Southern Railway main-line EMUs. By the early 1970s they were chiefly to be found on the Sussex coast stopping services, working eastwards from Brighton to Eastbourne and Hastings and westwards to Portsmouth. By now the enthusiast fraternity had realized their historical importance, and they worked tours all over the Southern electrified network and, indeed, beyond over the former LNWR suburban lines to Watford, Euston and the North London line. When the last unit was withdrawn at the end of September 1972, the recently-formed Southern Electric Group was in a position to step in and buy unit No 3142. Other vehicles from 4COR sets were also preserved; we shall look at the preservation scene in the next chapter.

THE BLUEBELL PHENOMENON

The first time I ever visited the Bluebell Railway I travelled there by electric train. This was possible in the early days, for the Horsted Keynes to Haywards Heath line was still open and 2BILs operated it, continuing southwards over the East-bourne main line to Lewes, Seaford and Newhaven. One of course merely used the electric trains as a means of getting to the vastly more interesting steam relics; the bread upon which the jam was spread, the blank tape upon which the music was recorded. Who would have thought that a couple of decades later, large sums of money would be spent by large numbers of quite sane punters to gaze fondly upon and, perhaps, if lucky, ride in the last surviving and officially preserved 2BIL?

The Bluebell wasn't quite the first standard gauge railway to be preserved in this county — that honour falls to the Middleton Railway in Leeds — but it was certainly the first complete ex-British Railways branch which had operated both a goods and passenger service until closure to pass into private ownership. The Bluebell showed what was possible, and from its example an extraordinary number of preservation schemes have proliferated. Just as Britain introduced the steam railway to the world, so it has led the way in preserving it.

Lest jingoism become utterly rampant, I would hasten to add that perhaps in the early days if the enthusiast movement, and the railway authorities, had been a little more understanding of the historic importance of other forms of motive power and other aspects of railway operation, then some of the gaps in what has survived and are now apparent would have been filled. Which is not to say that we ought not to be immensely grateful for the remarkably comprehensive collection we have. The enthusiast movement also learned quickly — well fairly quickly — not to scorn modern methods of public relations and technology and that if it was to survive and prosper some aspects of the past were best forgotten. And perhaps, most important of all, the knowledgeable enthusiast has a vital part to play in supporting and promoting the notion of rail travel on the national and

Early days on the Bluebell Railway. LB & SCR 'E4' Class 0–6–2T No 463 Birch Grove, bought from British Railways in 1962, heads a Sheffield Park-bound train over grass-grown track.

international network as both a pleasurable and relaxing experience (well, usually) and from an environmental point of view an asset worth fighting tooth and nail for.

Back in the 1960s and early '70s, British Rail and the preservation movement regarded each other warily. There were some within British Rail who went out of their way to be small-minded and obstructive whilst there were enthusiasts who would have been quite happy to see the entire electric and diesel-operated network torn up so long as their little bit of steam railway prospered. Thank goodness the picture is so very different today. British Rail and the preservation industry — for such it has become — both realize how much they need and can benefit from each other's co-operation. The Bluebell Railway has generally taken an enlightened approach and it was fitting that when work began on its long-awaited northern extension from Horsted Keynes to East Grinstead in March 1988, Paul Channon, the Secretary of State for Transport, and Chris Green, Director of Network SouthEast, were among the invited guests.

The event was covered by Jim Palm of the BBC Radio programme 'Rail'. After referring to the recently electrified London to Oxted and East Grinstead line, and the provisions made by British Rail at the latter station for Bluebell Railway trains to connect with BR ones, Jim Palm asked Mr Green about the general state of affairs in his area. Commenting on the 15 per cent increase in rail travel on Network SouthEast — 'the demand is the biggest we have ever had in the history of railways' — he went on to talk about the refurbishment of the 'workhorse trains', basically the CIGs, BIGs and VEPs, many new ones, further electrification, the modernization of every station, the reopening and opening of others and a generally expanding Network SouthEast. It would have been unthinkable 20 years ago that a programme which was essentially about the preservation movement should, first of all, have attracted such a figure as Chris Green to speak on it and, secondly, that it would have been thought that many enthusiasts would have wanted to hear what he had to say.

The Secretary of State was actually in charge of the steam crane which laid the first panel of track. He described himself to Jim Palm as a 'railway enthusiast' who travelled a great deal by BR trains and who also found steam trains 'very romantic'. After the track-laying ceremony, a replica of the last BR train over the branch, a two-coach train hauled by BR Standard 2–6–4T No 80154, was run. The real No 80154 was the last engine built at Brighton works and was withdrawn and scrapped in 1966, but for the occasion sister engine No 80064 was renumbered.

The very first train run by the Bluebell Railway when it began operations on 7 August 1960 also consisted of two carriages. The engine was certainly of historic interest, it was *Stepney*, one of the famous 'Terriers', but the carriages were considered to be merely something for the patrons to ride in, and were picked virtually at random from the end of the long line of condemned vehicles stretching south-westwards from Horsted Keynes towards Haywards Heath. One was an LSWR carriage with a most complicated, and, in hindsight, fascinating history. The other was held to be highly ordinary for it was a 1929-built Maunsell corridor brake composite. Such carriages were still to be seen working all over the Southern Region in 1960 and similar vehicles made up much of the Brighton line electric units.

All of this was 30 years ago, and what was commonplace then certainly isn't now. The LSWR carriage No 390, a non-corridor third built in 1900 but lengthened and fitted with a new Lancing-built underframe by the Southern Railway in 1933, was soon to be seen as a most interesting vehicle. It took a bit longer for the Maunsell carriage, No 6575, to be appreciated, and in its early days on the Bluebell it was painted in a miserable and quite inappropriate shade of blue. However, as time went on, Maunsell carriages began to be prized and other preservation groups were happy enough to acquire much-butchered examples from departmental service. The Bluebell Railway has, of course, a marvellous array of steam engines, but there are those who think that it has made an even greater contribution to the preservation movement in its unique collection of carriages. It was, quite simply, first in the field and thus owns three Maunsell steam-

Maunsell-built corridor brake composite No 6575, built at Lancing in 1929 and superbly restored at Horsted Keynes for service on the Bluebell Railway.

Horsted Keynes in the summer of 1987 with Maunsell corridor brake composite No 6686 of 1935 which ended its BR service on the 'Night Ferry' in 1966, and high-capacity ten-compartment SECR non-corridor third No 1098 of 1922.

hauled carriages bought in running order straight from passenger service on BR. The Bluebell also acquired SECR and Southern Railway Bulleid-designed carriages in this manner, and when this source ran out got hold of some departmental vehicles which were still fairly intact and were reasonably easy to restore to original condition.

But to return to Maunsell No 6575. After serving the Bluebell well in its early days it was set aside. By the late 1970s, its true worth had come to be appreciated and in the late summer of 1981 it re-entered service. Many of us remembered Maunsell carriages in passenger service, but far fewer could recall them in their original, ornate livery of the 1920s and '30s. No 6575 in her gleaming olive green paintwork with black and yellow/orange lining out and black-shaded gilt lettering and numbers looked truly magnificent, a once everyday carriage whose time had finally come, the ugly duckling which had emerged as a glorious swan.

Perhaps even more spectacular was the transformation of No 1309. This is a 1935-built Maunsell open third which served ten years as a mobile office after withdrawal from passenger service in 1963. The Bluebell Railway bought her in 1973, and set about restoration in 1981. I travelled in her shortly after she went back into passenger service in September 1984. The varnished mahogany panelling positively glowed, the brass and copper work was a delight and if the moquette was BR style rather than the original jazz pattern, few would have realized it. No wonder No 1309 received the accolade 'Coach of the Year' from the Association of Railway Preservation Societies. Both Nos 1309 and 6575 and the third Maunsell carriage currently in service on the Bluebell, brake composite No 6686, which ended its BR service on the 'Night Ferry' in 1966, have Lancing-built underframes.

The only complete LB&SCR carriage which the Bluebell Railway has been able to acquire is the Directors' Saloon No 60. Built at Lancing Works in 1913 on six-wheel bogies, the Southern Railway did little to improve its appearance when they fitted new windows. However, this modernization probably ensured its survival as an inspection saloon into the 1960s. It came to the Bluebell railway in 1965 and is presently awaiting overhaul and restoration, hopefully to as near original condition as possible.

Other carriages of SECR origin or design which reside on the Bluebell often worked on the Oxted and Brighton lines in Southern Railway and BR days. These include the ten-compartment non-corridor thirds, Nos 971 and 1098, plain-looking, high-capacity, but beautifully constructed vehicles, which might well have been converted to electric multiple unit stock but never were, instead ending their days as strengthening vehicles on Oxted line rush-hour duties, often working with Maunsell and Bulleid carriages as they do today.

This is not the place to list and describe the Bluebell's astonishing array of locomotives, but we will pick out those which have a particular association with the Brighton line. Pride of place goes to No 473 *Birch Grove* primarily because, like the Maunsell carriages, it was not the sort of machine which would ever have aspired to such an exalted position in its days as a workhorse of the LB&SCR, Southern Railway and BR. My chief memories of the Brighton radials are of shunting at Norwood and the now vanished yards of nearby stations, Thorton Heath, West Croydon and so on, and various odd jobs in the Brighton area. Their numbers helped fill up my *ABC*, but that was about the only use I had for such grubby, nameless antiques.

No 473 came out of Brighton works in 1898 and spent its early years at New Cross, later moving to Brighton. Like a number of the class in British Railways days, No 32473 came back to London, to work in alien — by a few yards — territory out of Nine Elms, the former LSWR shed which provided motive power for West of England, Bournemouth and Weymouth, and South-ampton ocean liner expresses. No 32473 was not untouched by all this glamour, for its duties chiefly involved hauling the empty carriages of such trains to and from the yards at Clapham Junction. The 'E4' was bought direct from British Railways by the Bluebell Railway, was repainted in Marsh's umber livery, and worked for nearly ten hard years. A long wait for overhaul ended in 1984, and the time is now not far away when the sole survivor of the many varieties of radial tank which served the Brighton line for so long will again steam through the Sussex countryside.

Right *Former SECR 'P' Class 0–6–0T No 27 and former LB & SCR 'E4' Class 0–6–2T Birch Grove double-head a train on the Bluebell Railway in the spring of 1972.*

Far right *Bulleid Class 'Q1' 0–6–0 No 33001 pulling out of Sheffield Park in 1983.*

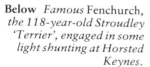

Below *Famous Fenchurch, the 118-year-old Stroudley 'Terrier', engaged in some light shunting at Horsted Keynes.*

The Bluebell's two 'Terriers' are the most famous engines on the line. No 55 *Stepney* wears Stroudley's gorgeous yellow ochre livery, as it did when it first emerged from Brighton works in 1875. It served as a main-line engine for no fewer than 85 years before inaugurating the standard gauge preservation movement in this country on 7 August 1960 when it hauled the Bluebell Railway's first public train. No 72 *Fenchurch* holds several records. It was the very first 'Terrier' to enter service, on 9 September 1872, and for 13 years from 1950 was the oldest locomotive at work on British Railways. As long ago as 1898, *Fenchurch* was sold out of main-line service, though it didn't leave Sussex, being bought by the Newhaven Harbour Company. Here it shunted up and down the quayside, a task it found so congenial that it pursued it for no fewer than 65 years. It had come back into main-line ownership when the harbour company was absorbed into the Southern Railway in 1923. In 1963, the western breakwater line at Newhaven was closed, thus ending the picturesque spectacle of No 32636, as *Fenchurch* had become, rumbling across the wooden bridge which also carried all road traffic. *Fenchurch* was immediately bought by the Bluebell Railway and today fittingly wears the lined black livery of the Newhaven Harbour Company, carrying that title on one tank side and *Fenchurch* on the other.

The Wainwright-designed 0–6–0 No 592 and 0–4–4T No 263 of the SECR are the sole representatives of classes which were not only long familiar on the Oxted line but were also often found working in and out of Brighton; 'H' Class locomotives, like the LSWR 'M7s', proved ideal for push-pull work and were to be found on many Sussex branch lines. No 31263, as the 'H' was numbered in BR days, worked the very last steam-operated former LB&SCR branch, that between Three Bridges and East Grinstead. Three Bridges shed closed on 4 January 1964, and the 'H' was bought for preservation later that year.

Of the Southern Railway-built engines, No 928 *Stowe* is perhaps the most glamorous. The 40 locomotives of the 'Schools' Class were the finest which Maunsell produced. The most modern and most powerful 4–4–0s in England, they won the hearts of enginemen wherever they worked. Never particularly numerous on the Central Section, they nevertheless performed briefly on London to Brighton expresses when new, and always had a few duties which regularly took them over former LB&SCR metals. After the Kent coast electrification, *Stowe* was often to be seen working the 16.40 fast from London Bridge to Brighton via Oxted and Uckfield. Upon withdrawal, No 928 was bought by Lord Montagu of Beaulieu, was later moved to the

East Somerset Railway and then came to the Bluebell Railway in 1980. Although *Stowe* had not steamed for 17 years, it was in good condition and soon entered service.

The two 0–6–0s — the 'Q' Class No 541, and the 'Q1' No 33001 — are once again representatives of types familiar in former LB&SCR territory, although both perform vastly more passenger work than they used to. The 'U' Class No 1618 was built at Brighton in 1928, although the unrestored sister engine, No 1638, came from Ashford. Maunsell 'Moguls' were amongst the most familiar of engines on both goods and passenger work on the Brighton line from the 1920s until the end of steam, and although the 'Ns' were more common than the 'Us', No 1638 worked many duties which brought it on to Brighton metals.

No 21C123 *Blackmoor Vale* is one of the few preserved Bulleid 'Pacifics' entitled to wear Southern Railway livery, for it was built at Brighton in 1946. It worked mostly on the Eastern and Western sections but is representative of a class which had charge of the final passenger workings on the Central section, particularly the Brighton to Plymouth train in the winter of 1966–7. *Blackmoor Vale* is yet another Bluebell engine which was bought direct from British Rail, although it did not reach Bluebell Railway metals until 1971.

No class has closer associations with the Central Section of the Southern Region in the last days of steam than the BR Standard 2–6–4Ts which were designed and built at Brighton. Initially, one tried to dislike them on account of the many old favourites — the 'I3's and the 'Pacific' tanks and, finally, the 'Atlantics', for example — whose demise they had caused, but nothing lasts for

Preserved 'U' Class 2–6–0 No 1618, built at Brighton works in 1928 and withdrawn from Guildford in 1964, basks in the sun at Horsted Keynes in the summer of 1988. A wooden-post LB & SCR lower quadrant semaphore signal is in the foreground.

No 1618 heads for Horsted Keynes in November 1988, running without smoke deflectors as originally built.

ever and the Standards were such handsome machines, powerful, free-running, and usually kept pretty clean, that it was impossible not to like them. The last was built only three years before the Bluebell Railway opened for business, and one doubts if a BR Standard 2–6–4T was high on anyone's list of priorities in 1960. However, in the fullness of time such a locomotive was seen to be a highly desirable property for the Bluebell and so there are now two on the line, the unrestored No 80100 and No 80064, which was first steamed on the Dart Valley Railway and shortly transferred to Sussex, its natural home.

The 999 BR Standard locomotives had a strong family likeness. They were nothing like as revolutionary as Bulleid's designs, although, or rather consequently, a good deal less troublesome. One of my favourites was the Class '4' 4–6–0. They were designed at Brighton and built at Swindon, and Three Bridges was allocated a batch which became the first and only 4–6–0s ever to work regularly over the Oxted line. Like the Standard tanks, the Bluebell's example, No 75027, was not actually employed on the Oxted line, but that's a minor point. For much of its BR career it was a Western Region engine. Now Swindon, naturally enough, was far more generous with its application of mid-chrome green than other works, and whilst the Southern Region Class '4s' wore lined black livery, No 75027 was given the full treatment and painted in what was basically GWR colours, although Swindon could not quite bring itself to provide a copper-capped chimney. As it happened, No 75027 finished up at Carnforth on the London Midland region, now Steamtown, and was working until the very last day of BR steam, 3 August 1968. Bought direct from BR, the Standard 4–6–0 came to Sussex in 1969 and has proved one of the Bluebell's most reliable and hard-working locomotives.

BR Standard '4MT' 4–6–0
No 75027 at Sheffield Park
on a wet spring day in 1988.

PRESERVATION
ELSEWHERE

The Bluebell has, of course, preserved a lot more than just locomotives and carriages. It has an LB&SCR milk van and many goods vehicles, one stuffed dog which in life collected money for railway charities, a splendid array of signalling, a museum, archives, and two interesting stations. The station house at Sheffield Park is a fine example of a typical mid-Victorian Wealden tile-hung villa, whilst Horsted Keynes is a surprisingly extensive junction set in the heart of rural Sussex.

However, it should not be thought that the Bluebell Railway has a monopoly of Brighton line preservation, although it was an extraordinary stroke of luck for LB&SCR *aficionados* that it came into existence when it did and thus acquired so much. Only the GWR, with its Great Western Society at Didcot, and the Severn Valley Railway in Worcestershire and Shropshire, has fared as well.

A fairly recent arrival on the scene has been Isfield station, between Uckfield and Lewes, which has been expertly restored, track relaid and steam trains re-introduced, although, inevitably, it was too late to acquire and run genuine former LB&SCR or Southern Railway locomotives and carriages. The Mid-Hants and the Kent and East Sussex Railways both have locomotives and carriages associated with the Brighton line and we have already looked at the Isle of Wight Steam Railway which is unique in that on it one may regularly travel in LB&SCR-built carriages hauled by an LB&SCR-built engine. 'Terriers' have gone far and wide in preservation, and one of their larger brothers, a Stroudley 'E1' Class 0–6–0T, is at Cranmore on the East Somerset Railway. This is No 110, built at Brighton in 1877, and subsequently sold on into industrial service where it managed to outlast all its main-line relations. Somewhat modified over the years, it is now being restored to LB&SCR condition.

Books have been written on the many Pullmans associated with the Brighton line, but of particular interest to us is the Brighton Locomotive Works. After the Pullman works at Preston

Preserved Stroudley 'E1' Class 0–6–0T being attended by a steam crane engine at Cranmore and showing signs of both Cannock & Rugeley Colliery and BR ownership, although the smokebox number is ficticious for she was never a British Railways engine.

Park closed down, the buildings were used for some years to store exhibits belonging to the National Collection. Occasionally, some of them would be wheeled out on public display, and the very last main-line steam engine, No 92220 *Evening Star*, once appeared at Brighton station, although not in steam. Eventually these exhibits were transferred elsewhere and now the former Pullman headquarters has become the Brighton Locomotive Works.

A more appropriate title would be 'Railway Works', for amongst those which have taken up residence is the Southern Electric Group, which owns the 4COR unit No 3142, bought from British Rail in 1972. There was at the time nowhere on the Southern Region to keep the unit, and so it was exiled to the Nene Valley Railway near Peterborough where it was sometimes most incongruously, but intriguingly, attached to one of that railway's mainland European steam locomotives. With the setting up of the Brighton works, it came back home and a most thorough restoration is now under way in the hope that it will once again be seen running over the third rail system.

The National Collection somewhat belatedly came to appreciate the historical importance of the Southern Railway EMUs and has preserved one of the 2BILs, No 2090. This is kept in working order at Lovers Walk depot, Brighton, and most happily appears at various open days regularly providing the opportunity to sample the delights of riding in a first generation main-line Southern EMU, usually attached to preserved 4SUB No 4732.

One is gratified that a representative of these latter stalwarts of the Southern suburban scene has also been kept for posterity, but I have been bounced about rather too many times between Thornton Heath and Victoria and elsewhere over the years in 4SUBs to go out of my way to repeat the experience. A 1925 3SUB motor coach is also preserved and on display at York, as is 4COR motor coach No 11179 from 4COR unit No 3131.

But back to Preston Park. Alongside the 4COR are two 'Brighton Belle' motor cars, Nos 92 and 93. There could, of course, be no more appropriate home for them, and work is proceeding on their restoration. As we have seen, all the former 'Brighton Belle' cars still exist and there are those who dream of the day when the 'Brighton Belle' will once again run over its old, familiar route. To some it is more than a dream. There are many obstacles to overcome, not the least being the absence of motors in any of the cars. However, it would be possible to replace them with EPB equipment and, given some of the extraordinary achievements of the preservation movement, the return of the 'Brighton Belle' is surely a possibility.

A 2BIL at the rear of a Victoria-Bognor semi-fast heads south into the teeth of a blizzard at East Croydon in January 1971.

Standing on the same track as the two 'Belle' motor cars is one of those freak survivals which makes one rub one'e eyes in disbelief. It is 'Balmoral', an 1883 Pullman sleeping car, built, like all the early Pullmans, in the USA. It was originally a six-wheeler, but was pretty uncomfortable in this state and was soon fitted with bogies. It ran first on the Great Northern Railway, then on the Highland and after the First World War was sold to become a bungalow at Seaford, along with its brother, 'Culross', and thus it survived. Both cars had, of course, their running gear removed, but the bodywork of 'Balmoral' was found to be in surprisingly good condition with much of the original engraved glass intact. It, and the remains of 'Culross', were brought to Preston Park in 1987.

Very nearly the most recent Brighton line preservation has been that of Class '71' electric locomotive No E5001. Built at Doncaster between 1958 and 1960, the 24 members of the class were a development of the three early Southern main-line electric locomotives. They were not entirely successful, being superseded by the Class '73' electro-diesels which had the ability to run, albeit at reduced power, over non-electrified track, which meant they could shunt in yards and venture beyond the third rail network. Some of the Class '71s' were converted to electro-diesels but were unreliable and the class had gone by the early 1980s. They are probably best remembered for hauling the Newhaven boat train, the 'Golden Arrow' and the 'Night Ferry'.

Do stations still in use on the BR network belong in a chapter devoted to preservation? If they are as historic and as splendid as Brighton, then I think they do. Vandals are not only to be found spraying aerosol cans at the yellow fronts of multiple units. Higher-placed 'vandals' can cause vastly longer-lasting damage to the environment when they plan the totally unnecessary destruction of splendid buildings, as they very nearly did for Brighton station in the 1970s.

At Easter 1973, British Rail and the Peachey Property Corporation published their plan to demolish the magnificent iron and glass roof of Brighton station and replace it with a 550-room hotel and lots of other mouth-watering facilities such as 5.4 acres of flats and an 'all-weather reception centre' — wow! As is sometimes the case, very little time was allowed for objections, but the ever-vigilant Brighton Society got together an excellent case, pointing out that the vast size of the development would dwarf its surroundings, and that Fred Bannister's 1882 station sheds were a listed building. The *fait accompli* which BR and Peachey had fondly anticipated was prevented, and in the event the development never took place.

'Brighton Belle' third class motor Pullmans Nos 92 and 93 under restoration at the former Pullman works at Preston Park in June 1988.

'Balmoral', a six-wheel Pullman built in 1883 for the GNR, rebuilt with bogies and eventually brought to Sussex as a seaside bungalow at Seaford at the end of the First World War. The body was rescued in 1987 and is seen in the works at Preston Park undergoing restoration in the summer of 1988.

Brighton station – the concourse in 1988.

Rather different are the arguments over the canopy covering the cab rank. In 1982, in the Brighton Station Development Area proposals, the East Sussex and Brighton Councils were still wittering on about the canopy 'which detracts from the original designs' as though the mere fact that something was original guaranteed its aesthetic purity. Certainly the façade is handsome, but then so is the canopy, and its usefulness cannot be denied. Today, both station and canopy look to be in pristine condition. One hopes that all half-baked, as well as downright evil, threats to what is surely the finest and liveliest seaside station in the land have finally been thwarted.

TODAY

So where does that leave the Brighton line today? How many people travel on it? Lots — lots and lots, they always did and still do.

I write this a few days after spending a Bank Holiday in Brighton. My wife and I sat drinking espresso coffee in a cafe in Queen Street 100 yards due south of the station opposite a large picture of George Melly wearing one of his purpose-built suits, listening to Glenn Miller, and watching a constant procession of people proceeding purposefully seawards. The vast hordes which used to pour down early in the morning and then queue up late in the evening to bounce back in wooden-bodied non-corridor carriages, briefly released, like their passengers, from the grimy suburbs, may be no more. But trains still arrive every few minutes, disgorge large numbers of clients — rather fewer in complete family groups, perhaps — but the important thing is that they keep coming throughout the day. And they don't just come from London. We had arrived on a train from Exeter which drew in beside one from Bedford. The notion of being able to stroll down the station at Bedford or Luton secure in the knowledge that within 20 minutes at the most an electric train

Brighton station in June 1988. Electro-diesel No 73101 Brighton Evening Argus *and Thameslink EMU No 319023 having just arrived from Bedford a few days after the inauguration of the through north-south Snow Hill tunnel route.*

will draw in which will then convey one direct to Brighton would have caused even the most far-seeing director of the Midland or LB&SCR companies to rub his eyes in disbelief.

From the beginning, the Brighton line has carried large numbers of workers — city gents, grooms, dockers, farm hands, students, secretaries, school children, social workers, property developers, air hostesses, fuller's earth excavators, night club hostesses, housewives, film stars, comic strip writers to name but a few. In the mid-1960s, Haywards Heath overtook Brighton in the league table of season ticket holders, although both were comfortably ahead of East Worthing's 13. At the last count, the average number of season ticket holders of all sorts travelling to all destinations — not just London, although that of course was the destination of the vast majority — was 2,210 from Brighton, 780 from Hassocks, 2,520 from Haywards Heath and 875 from Three Bridges.

In the late 1950s and early 1960s, some of the London-based insurance companies began to move their head offices out to the tower blocks which were just beginning to appear in Croydon. Hardly before we local inhabitants realised what had happened, we found ourselves living in what looked like a fair impersonation of Manhattan, though, unfortunately, without any of its compensations but with gales regularly howling through the wind tunnels which had been created. Croydon was never the most beautiful of county boroughs — it once tried to become a city but had its knuckles smacked for impertinence — but I can't say it was improved. Many regretted the passing of my old Whitgift Middle School with its oasis of green fields in the heart of the town where some of the senior citizens would come to watch the cricket, but all the changes certainly generated business for the railway and presently some 5,580 season tickets are bought each year, which means that it outstrips all the other stations, including the busiest of them all, Clapham Junction, which sells only 4,200.

Clapham Junction saw the very last steam-hauled branch line service on the Southern Region, a most curious distinction for a station which had been a hub of electrification since the First World War. It ran over the West London railway to Kensington Olympia, largely for postal workers although anyone could use it. I once travelled behind an 'H' Class tank, but at the end, in 1967, Standard 2–6–4Ts were in charge. The service still runs today with Class '33' diesel-electric locomotives.

These latter — the 'Cromptons' — with bodywork by the Birmingham Railway Carriage and Wagon Company, the makers of many Pullmans, first appeared on the Central section in

1960. Together with the Class '71' electric locomotives and the Class '73' electro-diesels they took charge of practically all non-multiple unit workings, both passenger and freight. The '71s' were fairly short-lived but the '33s' and '73s' are still a familiar sight on the Brighton line, although many of the former have been withdrawn.

The first of the electro-diesels, the '73s', came out in 1962. With their ability to work over non-electrified lines, albeit at considerably reduced power, they have proved immensely useful. Box-like in shape, in order to conform with the restrictions which 40 years earlier had caused the boiler mountings of former LB&SCR locomotives to be cut down so that they could work off their own lines, they look vastly better today in the much bolder liveries introduced in the 1980s.

The Oxted line had long been promised electrification. Hopes rose when it was seen that the steam era was coming to a close in the early 1960s, but were once again thwarted. Comfortable Bulleid and BR standard corridor carriages were replaced by noisy three-car diesel-electric multiple units without corridor connections. Whilst the Uckfield to Lewes line was still open these units worked regularly into Brighton, and even after it was closed they used to come down the main line as far as Keymer Junction where they turned left for St Leonards. A depot for servicing diesel-electric units had been opened here when dieselization came to the former SER Hastings line in 1957, but it

One of the original high-capacity Bulleid 4SUBs of 1944-5 passing a Class '33' in charge of a stone train from Ardingly near Clapham Junction in the summer of 1971.

The inauguration of the Oxted line electrification on 27 September 1987. A view from the cab of No 33008 Eastleigh *giving rides up and down the sidings with newly named No 73004* Bluebell Railway *in the bay platform.*

BR 4536/1

CELEBRATING THE
ELECTRIFICATION OF THE
EAST GRINSTEAD LINE
Valid for unlimited travel between
East Croydon and East Grinstead on
Sunday 27th September 1987.

FARE £1·00 **NOT TRANSFERABLE**
Issued subject to the regulations and
conditions in the publications and notices
of the British Railways Board.

Network SouthEast

seemed an awful waste of fuel and time for the Oxted units to travel so far on non-revenue journeys.

At long last electrification did come to the line, and on a Sunday in September 1987 I made quite sure I was there to help celebrate. BR, or Network SouthEast as it had then become, did everyone proud. There were exhibitions and events at every station. A Romney, Hythe and Dymchurch Railway engine steamed up and down the car park at Upper Warlingham, I rode in the cab of the Class '33' *Eastleigh* through the sidings at Oxted and took a photograph of 'P' Class 0–6–0T *Bluebell* on a low-loader at East Grinstead. Immaculate 4CIG units, in the latest livery, ran every quarter of an hour between East Croydon and East Grinstead, a £1 ticket covered as many journeys as you liked, and I savoured the experience of sitting in a corner seat of a first class compartment whilst gliding effortlessly through the many tunnels which take the line beneath the North Downs without any of the fuss and racket which the old diesels kicked up. It was a pity a strong enough case could not have been made for electrifying the Hurst Green to Uckfield line, but it is being resignalled and its future looks secure.

After many threats, the line from Eridge through Tunbridge Wells West to Tunbridge Wells Central closed in 1987. The handsome station buildings at the West station were gaslit until the end, and it would have been a tragedy if they had been demolished; however, a preservation group is campaigning strenuously to re-open the line and the odds are that it will succeed.

There has been a dramatic change in the pattern of services on the main line during the 1980s. Although the long familiar pattern of fast, semi-fast and slow trains between Victoria and London Bridge and Brighton continues, on top of this has been imposed, since 1984, the quarter-hourly 'Gatwick Expresses', composed of air-conditioned Class '488' sets powered by Class '73' electric locomotives, and, since 1988, the Brighton to Bedford Class '319' Thameslink electric multiple units. These might be said to have brought the overhead back to the Brighton, for they are dual purpose and work on that system north of London, switching to third rail when they reach Southern territory.

Matthew Engel was wittily scathing in the *Guardian* about the opening of the Thameslink service, starting off by referring to it as 'a noble enterprise' but ending after 'a succession of minor disasters' culminating in an 82 minutes late arrival at Brighton with a quote from a guard on the new trains, 'Without being too technical about it, they're crap'.

I asked Jim Palm, who also travelled on the first day, what his

experience was and he had a quite different story to tell: cheap introductory fares, although not widely advertised, trolley refreshment service working well and a punctual arrival. Basically the new trains are excellent and have been well patronized, but BR does have a habit of shooting itself in the foot by not getting its act together properly before introducing a new service, and, like the Wessex Electrics which began on the same day, there were far too many delays and mishaps in the first few weeks most of which could, and should, have been avoided.

The two London termini have also seen considerable changes. London Bridge needed drastic rebuilding after its Second World War battering and consequent neglect, but it wasn't until the 1980s that the job was done. A vastly improved station resulted with a spacious concourse — I bought several postcards of the Crystal Palace at an antique collectors' fair held in it one Saturday — covered waiting areas for buses and taxis, and excellent refreshment rooms.

The London stations have always been prime sites for development, and, with the subsidy to British Rail drastically slashed, the temptation to remove some of the magnificent train sheds and build tower blocks over the tracks has been great. It nearly happened at Brighton, it did happen at Birmingham New Street, and the result was total disaster. Victoria has gone a little way down the slippery slope. The concourse has not been touched, thank goodness — in fact, it has been enlarged — but long ago a check-in terminal was built for Gatwick Airport passengers over several of the platforms. A much greater project has been the 360,000 square feet of office space created over the Brighton line platforms and completed in 1989. Inevitably this has made the platform areas nearest the concourse very dark, although reflective tiles and strong artificial lighting are some compensation, and the shopping centre above, with escalator links to the concourse, is certainly attractive.

Royalty and heads of state no longer arrive in Pullmans from the Channel ports but they still come to Victoria in special trains from Gatwick Airport and make the short ceremonial journey to Buckingham Palace.

The news cinema, where I once saw Laurel and Hardy re-open the Romney, Hythe and Dymchurch Railway after the Second World War, situated above the taxi entrance leading from Buckingham Palace Road has gone, but the tiled map of the LB&SCR system beside the booking office remains, as do the *bureau de change*, the souvenir shops and the little cafes around the bus station in this most cosmopolitan of London stations.

Sometimes, when I was a student porter at Victoria in the early 1960s, I would work nights. When we had finished sweeping the concourse and generally tidying up after the last train had gone — there were no all-night Gatwick services in those days — the

The Victoria Centre.

St James's Park circa 1900
(Author's collection).

station was locked up for a couple of hours and we would slope off and find an empty carriage and get our heads down, usually in a Bulleid Oxted line three-car set. It was midsummer, and at around 5 am dawn would begin to break.

One morning I found it impossible to sleep. I got up, strolled across a deserted Victoria Street, past the Victoria Palace, for long the home of the Crazy Gang, down a side street and into St James's Park. I'd always thought this, with its lake and pelicans and view of Buckingham Palace and the Whitehall pinnacles above the trees, the most pleasant of central London's many open spaces. The sun was not yet visible but it was getting steadily lighter. A lone bird began to sing and then, almost as though commanded by a conductor, from every treetop bird-song burst forth. I had never until that moment quite believed in the dawn chorus — certainly I doubted that one moment there could be virtual silence and the next so much sound. But there could, and there was.

Although I have passed through Victoria Station a thousand and more times since then, I have never had the opportunity to repeat that magical experience. A Surrey or Sussex woodland could not have surpassed the variety and freshness of what must still take place every summer morning just a few yards from the West End terminus of the Brighton railway.

INDEX